THE LABYRINTH EXPERIENCE

AN EDUCATOR'S RESOURCE

© LORRAINE VILLEMAIRE, SSJ, MA

SISTERS OF ST. JOSEPH OF SPRINGFIELD, MA

S·E·E·D

This book is dedicated to the members of the SEED Committee and

those who supported the publication of this book.

Maureen Charest

Irene Comeau

Cathy Coyne

Patricia Curran

Constance Daub

Doris Harland

Karen Hurd

Ann Lynch

Sally Marsh

Irene Mizula

Roberta Mulcahy

Winifred Roulier

Nancy Welsh

Denise Granger

Editing, Mary Clare Finn

INTRODUCTION

The Labyrinth Experience: An Educator's Resource, is an invaluable book to introduce the labyrinth walk to students of all ages. It provides a broad scope of information for educators to implement labyrinth walks in multiple settings.

Its unique feature is that chapters naturally fall into three segments: information about labyrinth themes, the integration of related-academic subjects and an inclusion of labyrinth walk celebrations.

1. Labyrinth Themes

> A History of the Labyrinth
> The Labyrinth — A Metaphor for Life's Journey
> How to Walk the Labyrinth
> Labyrinth and Maze Designs
> Sacred Geometry
> How to Walk a Finger Labyrinth
> The Technique of Dowsing
> Constructing a Seven-Circuit Labyrinth
> Labyrinth Walk Celebrations

2. Integration of Related-Academic Subjects

> Music, Art, Language Arts, Science, Biology, Math, History, Social Studies, Poetry, Earth Science, Health Education, Mythology, Writing Skills and Problem Solving

3. Labyrinth Walk Celebrations

> Self-Esteem
> Positive Thinking
> Relaxation
> Peace

The purposes of integrating the labyrinth experience with academic subjects are to show the practical connections between labyrinth walks and their application to daily life, to increase interest in all academic subjects and to enhance the joy of learning through creative projects, games and exercises. Labyrinth walks foster growth in self-esteem, respect, positive thinking and relaxation. Surely this book is a unique approach to the mystery and wonder of the labyrinth.

Lorraine Villemaire has a BA in English and an MA in Education. She is certified in Elementary Education and as a Superintendent-Director of Vocational High School, with over forty years of teaching and curriculum development experiences on all levels of education. Her book, *Grammar and Writing Skills for the Health Professional,* was published through Delmar/Cengage Learning and is in its second edition. Lorraine is presently a certified labyrinth facilitator conducting labyrinth walks in prisons, retreat centers, community centers, churches of all denominations, park services and schools from pre-K through college throughout Western Massachusetts.

CHAPTER OUTLINE

CHAPTER 3 – HOW TO WALK THE LABYRINTH

CHAPTER 4 – LABYRINTH AND MAZE DESIGNS

CHAPTER 8 – LABYRINTH WALK CELEBRATIONS

CHAPTER 1

A HISTORY OF THE LABYRINTH

INTRODUCTION AND PERFORMANCE OBJECTIVES

History is the story of events and peoples who lived before the present time. Everything has a history that gives rise to ideas and events that are changed or modified over the years. Some occurrences are forgotten for years, decades or even centuries, only to reappear later. History is a process that tells about events leading to the present, building on the shoulders of those who came before us. In this sense, history is the beginning of our own story.

The word history is from the Greek language meaning inquiry. It later came to mean a written account. However, history is more than a retelling of events or memorizing facts. To know about history is one thing; to ask why things occurred in history is to search for the truth.

At the completion of this chapter, students will:

- trace the development of labyrinths throughout ancient history, the Middle Ages and modern times.

- appreciate the contribution history has made to our present knowledge and understanding of the labyrinth movement and its rich tradition.

- compare some historical and social factors with modern day living.

ANCIENT HISTORY

For a civilization to have a history, there must be written documentation, which is also true of the labyrinth. The actual time of the first appearance of the labyrinth is hard to determine, because people couldn't write at the time. Much of the information is fragmented and sometimes contradictory.

The earliest reliable data from history show that the design was found mainly on pottery, clay tablets, roof tiles, coins, stones, graffiti and rocks in Southern Europe, dating back to 4,500 to 4,000 BCE. The oldest labyrinth design that survived was a rock carving in an underground tomb in Luzzanas, on the island of Sardinia about 2,500 BCE.

Other early historical dates in the history of labyrinths are:

- 1800 BCE — First structure in Egypt.

- 1300 BCE — A ceramic vessel in Syria.

- 1200 BCE — Clay tablet in Greece.

- 750 BCE — Rocks in Spain.

- 1000 CE — Stones in China and Italy.

In Greece and throughout the Mediterranean, the seven-circuit design became the common labyrinth symbol used in most places prior to the first century.

A coin from Knossos, Crete, depicts the labyrinth on one side with Theseus and the Minotaur on the back, found in the third century BCE.

A clay tablet from Mycenaean Palace at Pylos in Southern Greece is inscribed with a labyrinth in 1250 BCE, possibly a doodle.

This picture of a Etruscan wine jar from the 7th century BCE shows soldiers running from a labyrinth, with the word Troy written on the outer circuit.

This labyrinth pattern is different from the earlier model and represents a change in the original symbol. It is 2,000 years old.

The origin of the symbol is a mystery. Perhaps the legend of the labyrinth was preserved in the writings of famous Greek authors like Pliny and Homer. What is remarkable is that this symbol existed for centuries and was passed on from generation to generation and civilization to civilization.

The classical Greek and Roman cultures made magnificent contributions to civilization, particularly through mythology. A myth is a story associated with a person, institution or occurrence passed on to illustrate the struggles and achievements in the lives of people. Like the metaphor, a myth can be interpreted on two levels, the story itself and its deeper meaning. When interpreted by future generations, it invokes meaning and understanding to the present generation. Among the great Greek and Roman myths is the story of Theseus and the Minotaur and his experience with the labyrinth.

THESEUS AND THE MINOTAUR
A SYNOPSIS BY JANE BUCKMAN

The story of Theseus and the Minotaur is a classical Greek myth. It takes place on the Island of Crete and was recorded by Homer, Hesiod, Thucydides, Plutarch and others long after the Minoan culture ended. The ancient legend guided archeologists to search for this ancient civilization.

Zeus, who was smitten by Europa transformed himself, as the Greek gods so easily did, into a bull. The princess, who at the time was picking flowers, climbed on to the back of this beautiful bull. Zeus quickly plunged into the sea and carried her off to Crete. They gave birth to a son, Minos. Europa became princess of Phoenicia and later married Asterios who was the king of Crete. Minos eventually became the king of Crete.

King Minos lived in the Palace of Knossos with Queen Pasiphae, daughter of Helios the sun god. His rule came into question among his brothers, so he prayed to Poseidon to send him a bull as a sign that the throne belonged to him alone. As an offering for the sign, he promised Poseidon that he would sacrifice the bull.

A majestic bull appeared from the sea as the requested sign, but the bull was so magnificent that Minos could not bring himself to sacrifice it. Instead, he chose another bull as an offering in its place.

Poseidon wasn't a god to fool around with, so as an act of revenge, he caused the Queen to have an uncontrollable passion for the bull. The Queen had Daedalos, the ingenious craftsman, build a model of a cow, which she climbed into. The bull obviously was beautiful but dull-witted. From this union a son was born with the body of a man and the head and tail of a bull. King Minos, in order to hide this shame, had Daedalos build a tremendous labyrinth (maze) where the Minotaur was placed.

King Minos had won a battle at sea against Athens and as a tribute demanded that the Athenian king send seven boys and seven girls to be sacrificed to the Minotaur each year. Theseus, the son of the King of Athens, volunteered to be one of the fourteen youth sent to Crete. He was determined to kill the Minotaur and forever end the sacrifice of Athenian youth.

King Minos' daughter, Ariadne, fell in love with Theseus and was determined to help him. She acquired a skein of golden thread from Daedalos which Theseus tied to the entrance of the labyrinth — unwinding it as he penetrated the labyrinth to find the Minotaur. After a long and difficult journey, he finally reached the heart of the labyrinth and killed the Minotaur. He then found his way back out of the labyrinth by rewinding the ball of golden thread.

Theseus, taking Ariadne with him, escaped from Crete to return to Athens. They had an overnight stop on the island of Naxos where, for some unknown reason, he sailed away, leaving her asleep on the beach.

Not to worry though. The god Dionysos fell in love and married her. Together they had three sons.

In this tale, a man discovers his identity, heroically overcomes great obstacles and ends unjust human sacrifices. It may also be interpreted to represent the death of one empire into the rebirth of another, like so many empires over the course of history.

THE MIDDLE AGES (MEDIEVAL AGES)

The Middle Ages cover a span of years between the fall of the Roman Empire to about the middle of the 15th century. The period included feudalism, the Battle of Hastings, knighthood, castles, chivalry, the Black Death, Charlemagne, the aristocracy and much more. Two features of this era that particularly affected the culture of the labyrinth were the Crusades and the pilgrimage.

Religion was an important part of life in the Middle Ages. Men and women devoted their lives and much of their money to religious endeavors. A strong custom was to make a pilgrimage. A pilgrimage is a long journey made to a sacred space as an act of religious devotion. Pilgrimages were part of many different religions over the centuries.

- Hindus journeyed to India to bathe in the Ganges River.

- Muslims journeyed to Mecca.

- Christians journeyed to Jerusalem, Rome, Santiago De Compostela, Spain
  and the Canterbury Cathedral in England.

- Jews journeyed to Jerusalem to pray at the Wailing Wall.

The Crusades were wars between Christians and Saracens which occurred between 1096 and 1291. This period is known as the Hundred Years War. During the Crusades, it was dangerous for people to make pilgrimages.

In order to provide a more peaceful and safe pilgrimage, labyrinths were built on church floors as a substitute. The most famous cathedral with a pilgrimage labyrinth still existing today is at Chartres Cathedral in France, built around the year 1201.

The labyrinth design of the Middle Ages was more complex than the ones of the earlier centuries. The design still standing at Chartres is divided into four quadrants with a rosette design at the center. The labyrinth measures 42' in diameter. The distance from the entrance to the center is only 14', the length of the circular path is about a quarter of a mile. Millions of people walk this labyrinth yearly.

Between 1387 and 1400, the experience of making a pilgrimage was captured by one of the greatest writers in English literature, Geoffrey Chaucer. It contains stories of 30 people from all walks of life who made a pilgrimage to Canterbury, England and told tales about themselves as a means of entertainment. The book is titled, *The Canterbury Tales*.

The printing press was not invented yet so stories were written in manuscript form. The English language was very different in the Middle Ages than it is today. Compare the old English used in Chaucer's, *The Knight's Tale*, with modern English.

A Knight ther was, and that a worthy man,	A knight there was — and that a worthy man
That fro the tyme that he first bigan	That from the time that he first began
To ryden out, he loved chivalrye,	To ride to battle, he loved chivalry,
Trouthe and honour, freedom and curteisye.	Truth and honor, freedom and courtesy.
Ful worthy was he in his lordes werre,	Full worthy was he in his lord's war.
As wel in Cristendom as in hethenesse,	In both Christendom and in heathen places
And evere honoured for his worthinesse.	He was ever honored for his worthiness.
At Alisaundre he was whan it was wonne.	When Alexandria was won, he was there.

Prior to the modern era, labyrinths existed on most continents and in every major culture and religion. Labyrinths were found in Algeria, Brazil, Peru, Spain, Ireland, Italy, England, Scandinavia, Iceland, Greece, Egypt, Syria, and India.

MODERN TIMES

The labyrinth had special meaning to the people who walked it throughout past centuries. To the ancients, it was a time of rebirth. In the middle ages, it became a tool for pilgrimages. In modern times, it is a symbol of unity and peace with everything in the universe.

In the early history of our country, the first appearance of the labyrinth design originated from the Hopi Indians in Arizona. The symbol was a seven-circuit design representing Mother Earth and found on medicine wheels, woven baskets and ceremonial sticks. The Hopi tribe believed that humanity was connected with nature, the original source of life.

There were periods of decline of the labyrinth. It was forgotten for years only to reappear during times of economic prosperity, population growth and appreciation of nature. In the United States, the labyrinth began to make a comeback in the 1970s and 1980s, when it took off rapidly. Since then it has grown by quantum leaps. Their numbers are increasing, so much so that there are presently more labyrinths in the United States than any other part of the world. Like the visible part of an iceberg above water, the location of many labyrinths is well known. Like the invisible part of the iceberg below water, many labyrinth locations are unknown.

Why has the labyrinth become so popular? The desire to walk labyrinths comes from people's need to step out of the whirlwind of daily living anxieties and dis-ease in order to experience the healing and transformative power of the labyrinth.

Others believe the labyrinth is a tool for change, meditation, therapy and rehabilitation. Some are attracted to its universal appeal as a non-religious tool. As a result, there are currently labyrinths in hospitals and other health facilities, churches of all denominations, prisons, drug centers, youth detention centers, schools and private homes. They come in all sizes and shapes and can be created in hours, days, weeks or years. When building them, creativity knows no limits. Boston College created a memorial labyrinth placing names on stones of former graduates who died in the Twin Towers on 9/11.

Many pioneers are giving shape to the modern labyrinth movement. A few of them are Dr. Jean Houston, Helen Curry, Robert Ferre, Marty Cain, Helen Raphael Sands, Jeff Saward, Virginia Westbury, Marty Kermeen, and Alex Champion.

One person, among many who is instrumental in the revival of the labyrinth in the U.S., is Rev. Dr. Lauren Artress, an Episcopalian priest and psycho-therapist from Grace Cathedral in San Francisco, CA. While walking the labyrinth at Chartres, France in 1992, she felt called to build the design at Grace Cathedral. The cathedral now has both an indoor and outdoor labyrinth, each a replica of the medieval labyrinth at Chartres. Rev. Artress travels the world promoting the labyrinth and training people as labyrinth facilitators.

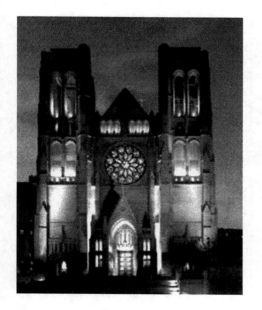

Many labyrinth organizations exist throughout the world. Rev. Lauren Artress is the founder of Veriditas, the Voice of the Labyrinth Movement, whose mission is to reintroduce the labyrinth as a spiritual tool. The Labyrinth Society is an organization of labyrinth enthusiasts from all over the world. Members seek to place labyrinths in schools and healthcare facilities. The Labyrinth Society and Veriditas created the World-Wide Labyrinth Locator, an easy-to-use database of international labyrinths. It contains information about labyrinths, their location, pictures and contact details. Lea Goode-Harris of the Santa Rosa Labyrinth Foundation wrote her doctoral thesis on exploring the significance of the labyrinth. She is like many enthusiasts who, "design, explore, live and breathe labyrinth". The present generation continues to build on the shoulders of those who previously walked the labyrinth path. The remaining chapters in this book elaborate on their contributions.

LABYRINTH HISTORICAL TIME LINE

4000 BCE
Design on rocks in Southern Europe.

2500 BCE
Oldest surviving labyrinth on the Island of Sardinia.

1800 BCE
Labyrinths discovered in Egypt.

1300 BCE
Labyrinths discovered in Syria.

1200 BCE
Labyrinths discovered in Greece.

1000 – 750 BCE
Labyrinths discovered in China, Italy and Spain.

3rd – 7th CENTURY
Labyrinth symbol found on coins in Crete.

MEDIEVAL - MIDDLE AGES
Labyrinths in Italy, France and Germany.

1200 - 1220
An 11-circuit labyrinth built in Chartres, France is still standing.

20th CENTURY
Revival of interest in labyrinths occurred.

MODERN LABYRINTH
Replica of Chartres labyrinth built at Grace Cathedral in San Francisco, CA.

POST MODERN
Organizations promoting world-wide interest in labyrinths.

LABYRINTH ORGANIZATIONS
Veriditas, The Voice of the Labyrinth Movement
Labyrinth Enterprise
Labyrinth Society
Santa Rosa Labyrinth Foundation
Caerdroia, Labyrinth Magazine
Labyrinth Resource Group

ACADEMIC INTEGRATION - HISTORY OF THE ANCIENT PYRAMIDS

The pyramids are the oldest and only surviving monument of its type in the ancient world. The largest, the Great Pyramid, was erected as a burial place for the Pharaoh Khufu. Scholars speculate that the sloping sides helped the soul of the pharaoh to reach the sky and the Gods. They are mentioned here because labyrinths were walked to get to the pyramid.

The Egyptians believed strongly that there was life after death. Pyramids were burial places or tombs to house and protect pharaohs in the after life. The structure was shaped like a triangle because it was an easier way to reach heaven and resist earthquakes, violent storms and other natural disasters.

Sometimes the pharaoh's wife was buried with him. Also buried were things that might be needed in the land of the dead. Passageways were made inside the pyramid to store gold, food, soldiers for protection and a boat to travel.

Everything about the structure is mammoth, an engineering feat unequaled even to this day. Consider these facts:

- HEIGHT – 81 feet high, as high as a 40 story building.

- LENGTH OF ONE SIDE – 755 feet or 1/7th of a mile.

- NUMBER OF BLOCKS – over two million.

- AREA COVERED – 13 acres or ten football fields.

- WEIGHT OF BLOCKS – 2 tons, the size of two cars.

- HEAVIEST BLOCK – 15 tons, one stone shaped every two minutes for 23 years.

- NUMBER OF WORKERS – hundreds of thousands.

- MATERIALS USED – granite and limestone from quarries.

Building the pyramid was difficult, back-breaking and dangerous work. If one stone fell, it could kill hundreds of workers. Many theories exist on how these huge memorials were made. The steps could have been like this:

1. Heavy blocks of granite and limestone from quarries were transported by boats across the Nile River to places where pyramids were built.

2. Stones were hauled on wooden rollers. Milk or water was poured over the rollers to help the blocks slide more easily.

3. Brick ramps were used to lift stones to heights where the work took place. Ramps were used on the sides of the pyramid.

What is amazing about the pyramids is that these great works of art were built without cranes or bulldozers. Some people say that even with modern technology, most of these treasures could not be built today. Is it any wonder that the great pyramid of Giza is called one of the Wonders of the World?

A MODERN PYRAMID

Pyramids are part of the architecture of the modern age. A large glass pyramid found in front of the Louvre Museum in Paris, the largest museum in the world, was completed in 1989. The Lourve pyramid was designed by a Chinese born American architect named I.M. Pei. It has a height of 70 feet, a square base of 115 feet and forms part of the new entrance to the museum.

Some people feel the pyramidal structure is too modern and looks out of place in front of the Louvre's classical architecture. Others believe it is a good comparison of the old and the new, the Classical and the ultra modern. The Louvre Pyramid was clearly featured in the movie *The Da Vinci Code*.

HISTORY PROJECT

Use the Labyrinth Historical Time Line as your guide and make a time line of your life, specifying events that were important in your life.

SOCIAL STUDIES – LIFE IN THE MIDDLE AGES

Knighthood was important in the Middle Ages. The role of knights was to protect people in villages, castles and during war. Because knights were clad in armor, they were hard to identify in battle. On the battlefield, knights had to know who was a friend and who was an enemy. It was a matter of life and death.

One way to solve this problem was for each knight to have a unique design on his shield unlike any other. Originally the design was called a badge, a word we still use today for identification.

A knight's tunic had the same design as his shield which later became known as a COAT OF ARMS. Men who designed a coat of arms were called heralds. Some designs were elaborate and others were very simple.

Special colors were used: silver, gold, blue, red, black, green and purple. The designs were very meaningful and told a lot about the knight and his family. When a daughter married the son of another family, the two coats of arms were combined and passed on from generation to generation. The coat of arms also appeared as flags over the castle.

Draw your own coat of arms. Include items that would identify you to others. See how many students you can identify from their coat of arms.

Compare the life style of the Middle Ages with the Modern Age. Write any similarity or difference in the right column. The first one is an example.

MIDDLE AGES	MODERN TIMES
1. Doctors believed disease was caused by too much blood in the body and used leechers to suck it out.	This practice was proven dangerous. In many instances now, blood is given to patients.
2. Girls could marry at age 12, boys at age 14. Marriages were arranged by parents.	
3. Titles and ranks mattered a great deal with no chance of moving up socially.	
4. Apprentices began to learn skills at age eight and lived with their trainer. After seven years, they became skilled workers.	
5. This was a time of great achievement in art, architecture, music, poetry and highly skilled arts.	

6. The Black Plague occurred in the Middle Ages and killed millions of people.	
7. Chess was a popular form of entertainment.	
8. There was a great contrast between the rich and the poor.	
9. During the Crusades, labyrinths were placed in cathedrals so people could make pilgrimages.	
10. Knights played the game of joust.	

LANGUAGE ARTS - WRITING ASSIGNMENTS

1. Study the lives of Hercules, Apollo, Tantalus and Prometheus in Greek mythology. Write how these myths apply to modern times.

_____

_____

_____

_____

_____

_____

_____

_____

2. Research the history of the Olympics and compare them to the Olympics of today.

_____

_____

_____

_____

_____

_____

_____

ART AND ACTIVITY ON THESEUS AND THE MINOTAUR

The myth of Theseus and the Minotaur is the subject of many works of art.

Theseus and the Minotaur, Athenian black-figure vase, 500 BCE.

A finger ring set in gold with a scene of Theseus slaying the minotaur. 1st century BCE.

When archaeologists uncovered the ruins at Knossos, they found this strange picture of young men jumping over a bull.

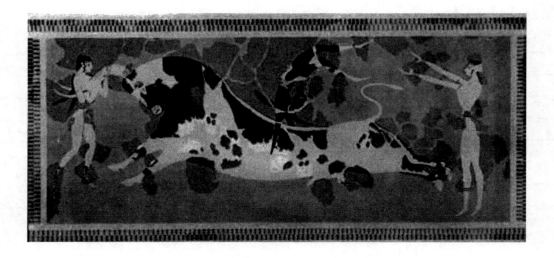

ACTIVITY

Hide a prize in a special area of your educational facility. Use yarn to assist someone to find it.

CHAPTER 2

THE LABYRINTH – A METAPHOR FOR LIFE'S JOURNEY

INTRODUCTION AND PERFORMANCE OBJECTIVES

Education is about making connections. For high school and adult students to understand and make the connection between the labyrinth and life's journey, it is necessary to understand the meaning of a metaphor and how to apply it to both their academic and personal lives.

At the completion of this chapter, students will:

- understand the meaning of the labyrinth and metaphor.

- make the connection between the labyrinth as a metaphor for life's journey.

- interpret the message of the metaphor and transfer it to daily living.

- recognize metaphors and similes in literature, poetry and art.

MEANING OF LABYRINTH

Labyrinth is a Greek word that means <u>path</u>. The labyrinth is a single, circular path embedded on flat ground or a floor surface that leads to a center and back out again, returning the same way.

What is special about walking the labyrinth is that it places the walker in the present moment. The gentle movement of putting one foot in front of the other enables the walker to become aware of what is happening in life right here and now, in this particular moment.

Consider some similarities between the labyrinth path and life's path:

- The labyrinth path, like many paths in life, has many twists and turns.

- Sometimes the direction of the path is very clear and sometimes it isn't.

- In both the labyrinth path and life's path, we encounter many people along the way, acknowledging them and moving on.

- The path may lead to an entirely different place than initially anticipated.

Because of these similarities, the labyrinth is often referred to as a metaphor for life's journey. Knowing what a metaphor is helps to understand this connection more clearly.

MEANING OF METAPHOR

Metaphor is a Greek word that means transfer. A metaphor is a writing tool or skill that uses words to:

- Compare one object or idea with another object or idea.

- Better understand or enjoy the message.

- Give greater meaning to something when there are no easy words to express or describe it.

- Transfer the meaning of a metaphor to daily activities.

EXAMPLE: His home is a <u>prison</u>.

In this sentence, prison is the metaphor and states that the person's home has some of the characteristics of a prison. Perhaps the person couldn't leave because of sickness, was forced to stay by another or was afraid to go outside. The reason is unclear. However, using a metaphor adds a lot more mystery, intrigue and feeling about the home environment. Metaphors enliven prose and convey a broad meaning in only a few words.

Metaphors are used in common everyday language to make sentences more interesting, alive and colorful. Consider the following:

METAPHOR	MEANING
The police <u>dug up</u> evidence.	Searched for facts.
America is a <u>melting pot</u>.	Many cultures mixed together.
The yard was a <u>blanket of snow</u>.	Snow evenly covers the ground.
Science is a <u>weighty subject</u>.	Difficult facts to learn.
The teacher was <u>boiling mad</u>.	Extremely angry.
Keep your eyes <u>peeled for any change</u>.	Examine closely, be watchful.
Let <u>sleeping dogs lie</u>.	Leave situations as they are.
Computers are <u>vehicles of information</u>.	Carry all kinds of data.
John is such a <u>couch potato</u>.	Always sitting or resting.
Complaining only <u>adds fuel to the fire</u>.	Makes matters worse, flares up.

METAPHORIC POEM

The following poem is a metaphor that compares family members to articles found in a medicine chest.

METAPHOR FOR A FAMILY

My family lives inside a medicine chest.

Dad is the super-size band aid, strong and powerful,

but not always effective in a crisis.

Mom is the middle-size tweezers

which picks and pokes and pinches.

David is the single small aspirin on the third shelf

sometimes ignored.

Muffin, the sheep-dog, is a round cotton ball,

stained and dirty,

that pops off the shelf and bounces

in my way as I open the door.

By Belinda, Family Education Network — Used with permission.

"All the world's a stage,

And all the men and women merely players,

They have their exits and their entrances."

William Shakespeare

"The wind was a torrent of darkness among the gusty trees.

The moon was a ghostly galleon tossed upon cloudy seas,

The road was a ribbon of moonlight over the purple moor,

And the highwayman came riding-

Riding—riding—

The highwayman came riding, up to the old inn-door."

Alfred Noyes

Metaphors are used in various types of literature: stories, poetry, fairy tales, parables, legends, ballads, plays and comic strips.

Myths, dreams and folktales are also metaphors that help readers receive the message the heart needs to hear. They reflect the human experience and help folks cope with what is happening in life.

METAPHORIC STORY

Most people are familiar with the story from Aesop's fables, *The Tortoise and the Hare*. This story shows a simple example of how a metaphor works. The hare challenges the tortoise to a race, bragging that he can easily win. Running way ahead of the tortoise, the hare stops by the wayside to rest but falls asleep, allowing the tortoise to overtake him and reach the goal first.

The story is about much more than a race. As a metaphor, it flourishes with many powerful messages:

- Slow and steady wins the race.

- Believe in yourself.

- Do your best with who you are and gain rewards.

- Hard work pays off.

- Stay focused.

- Think twice before bragging.

SNOWDROP

THE LABYRINTH PATH AS A METAPHOR FOR LIFE'S JOURNEY

Walking the labyrinth path, putting one foot in front of the other, is to experience a story about what is happening in life. The experience may surface a thought, idea, feeling, person, joy, sadness, memory, relaxing moment, problem solution, meaningful celebration or simply a pause to absorb the sounds of nature. Whatever surfaces during the walk becomes the metaphor. Once identified, the receiver transfers the metaphor's message into daily action.

LABYRINTH WALK METAPHOR EXAMPLE

John knew he needed his GED to succeed in life, yet he failed the science component of the GED test. His teacher told him how disappointed she was in him. She said he was a good student and failing should not have happened.

Later that day, John walked the labyrinth. As he circled the path, he felt uncomfortable and sad. It dawned on him that it was the poor science mark that concerned him. He didn't like science, it was a weighty subject. He thought that because he was a good student, he didn't have to apply himself as much. As John completed the walk, he knew he had to study harder and retake the test a second time and pass.

These questions help to identify the metaphor:

How did John feel while walking the labyrinth?

What life experience surfaced?

Describe the metaphor.

What is the message of the metaphor?

How did John transfer the message into daily action?

How was John transformed by the experience?

The dynamics of a labyrinth walk involve three simple steps: finding the metaphor, comparing it to a present life situation and transferring the lesson into daily living.

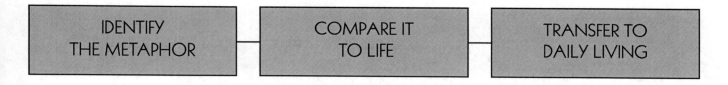

IDENTIFY THE METAPHOR — COMPARE IT TO LIFE — TRANSFER TO DAILY LIVING

Not every metaphor is as clear as this example. Insights may not immediately surface or may only come days later. Whatever happens, or doesn't happen becomes the metaphor. To walk for no reason at all is a breath of fresh air. Every labyrinth walk has a message even if it is simply to satisfy one's curiosity that the way out is the same as the way in. Every walk is a learning experience one way or another.

WALKING THE LABYRINTH IS A GIFT YOU GIVE TO YOURSELF.

Since education is about making connections, academic subjects of art, poetry, discussions, language arts and writing skills are integrated into this chapter.

ACADEMIC INTEGRATION - LANGUAGE ARTS – METAPHORS AND SIMILES

A metaphor and a simile are the best known types of figures of speech. Though they are often studied together as comparisons, they are different. As stated earlier in this chapter, a metaphor (from the Greek meaning transfer) is a comparison between two or more unrelated subjects. An <u>A</u> is compared to *B*.

      A   B

The <u>labyrinth</u> is a *bridge over troubled waters.*

A simile is a comparison using the words like, as or than. <u>A</u> is like *B*.

    A   B

<u>He</u> left *like a bolt of lightning.*

EXAMPLES OF SIMILES

busy <u>as</u> a bee   tough <u>as</u> leather

slow <u>as</u> a tortoise   two heads are better <u>than</u> one

ate <u>like</u> a pig   ate more <u>than</u> he could chew

The poem, *Metaphor for a Family,* was a metaphoric poem. The poem below is used as a simile.

CHOCOLATE CAKE

Friends are like chocolate cake, you can never have too many.

Chocolate cake is like heaven — always amazing you with

each taste or feeling.

Chocolate cake is like life with so many different pieces.

Chocolate cake is like happiness, you can never get enough of it.

Author Unknown

WRITING SKILLS ON THE METAPHOR AND SIMILE

Write a short explanation of these metaphors:

WALKING THE LABYRINTH GIVES PEOPLE AN OPPORTUNITY TO CHARGE THEIR BATTERIES.

_____
_____
_____
_____
_____
_____
_____
_____
_____
_____
_____
_____
_____
_____

AFTER THE LABYRINTH WALK, JOHN FELT AS LIGHT AS A FEATHER.

_____
_____
_____
_____
_____
_____
_____
_____
_____
_____
_____
_____

ART - ILLUSTRATION OF A METAPHOR

Divide the class into small groups. See how many metaphors each group can name in ten minutes. Compare answers.

Draw an illustration to convey the meaning of one metaphor mentioned in the chapter, group discussion or one of the following:

catch the game on TV	food for thought
plowed through the leaves	hitting his head against a wall
a new crop of students	an appetite for learning
a special place in your heart	my plate is already full
a caterpillar is an upholstered worm	

BIOGRAPHY OF PAUL CEZANNE

Paul Cezanne was born on January 19, 1839 in Aux-en-Province in southern France to an upper, middle-class family. His father was a banker and wanted his son to become a lawyer. Paul decided he would be an artist.

His art was not appreciated or well known by the public. Between 1860 and 1886, however, he gained recognition. Many described him as generous and tender, but also capable of unleashing an ugly nature. For an artist, Cezanne had a unique and likeable painting style.

In later years, Paul kept himself busy. He would rise early to paint in his studio. He enjoyed going for long walks in the countryside to receive inspiration.

In 1906, Aux was hit by a terrible heat wave and Cezanne found it hard to work under those conditions. One afternoon he was caught in the rain for hours and collapsed from fatigue. A few days later on October 22, Paul Cezanne died doing what he loved most, painting outside. Cezanne became known as the Father of Modern Art.

PAUL CEZANNE
SELF PORTRAIT

PAINTINGS BY PAUL CEZANNE

Look on the Internet for these pictures in color by Paul Cezanne.

Bend in Forest Road

A Bend in the Road

Notice how Cezanne uses broad strokes to create massive trees, rocks and bushes to envelop a road or path. The pictures clearly show the contrast between light and dark colors; tall, black tree barks overlapped with bright yellow, orange, blue and green. Both pictures invite the viewer to walk the road and discover what is around the bend.

How different or alike are these paths with the labyrinth path?

Cezanne took long walks in nature to gain inspiration. How can the labyrinth walk be a source of inspiration?

POETRY - BIOGRAPHY OF ROBERT FROST 1874 – 1963

Robert Frost was born in San Francisco. After his father's death in 1885, he moved with his family to Lawrence, Massachusetts where he became interested in reading and writing poetry while in high school. Frost attended Dartmouth College and Harvard University, but never received a degree. He was a jack-of-all trades and had many different occupations after leaving school; including a teacher, a cobbler and an editor of the local newspaper, *The Lawrence Sentinel*. His first poem, *"My Butterfly: An Elegy"* was published in the New York literary journal, *The Independent*, in 1894.

In the following years, he operated a farm in Derry, New Hampshire and taught at Derry's Pinkerton Academy. In 1912, he sold his farm and moved his family to England so he could devote himself entirely to his writing. His efforts to establish himself in England were immediately successful. In 1913, he published, "*A Boy's Will*", followed a year later by "*North of Boston*". It was in England where he met and was influenced by such poets as Rupert Brooke and Robert Graves and where he established his life-long friendship with Ezra Pound who helped to promote and publish his work.

Frost returned to the United States in 1915. By 1930 he was the most celebrated poet in North America. He was granted four Pulitzer Prizes. Robert Frost lived and taught for many years in Massachusetts and Vermont. He died on January 29, 1963 in Boston.

POEM - THE ROAD NOT TAKEN - By Robert Frost

Two roads diverged in a yellow wood,

And sorry I could not travel both

And be one traveler, long I stood

And looked down one as far as I could

To where it bent in the undergrowth.

Then took the other, as just as fair,

And having perhaps the better claim,

Because it was grassy and wanted wear;

Though as for that the passing there

Had worn them really about the same;

And both that morning equally lay

In leaves no step had trodden back.

Oh, I kept the first for another day;

Yet knowing how way leads on to way,

I doubted if I should ever come back.

I shall be telling this with a sigh

Somewhere ages and ages hence:

Two roads diverged in a wood, and I —

I took the one less traveled by

And that has made all the difference.

POEM DISCUSSION

The poem by Robert Frost, *The Road Not Taken*, is rather tricky to interpret and raises many questions. It begins with the poet trying to decide which path to take, knowing he couldn't travel both. The less traveled path is chosen, because it is, "grassy and wanted wear," but later the poet expresses that both paths are equally worn, "about the same", but still are not really the same. What is meant by this statement?

The poet feels sad because both paths can't be taken. Although he desires to walk the other path, he knows he won't pass this way again. Will he always wonder what he missed by not taking the other path?

Why do most people ask this question about their decisions?

What does the poet mean by, "yet knowing how way leads on to way?"

The poet's choice affects his future. How does he know the chosen path "made all the difference" since the future is not known until it is lived?

How do our decisions in life make a difference?

What does the poem say about self reliance and following one's own path rather than that chosen by another?

What are some of the choices people make while traveling the road of life?

How does one feel when he or she comes to a fork in the road and has to make a decision?

HOW DOES THE POET'S INITIAL VIEW OF THE PATH DIFFER FROM SOMEONE FACING THE OPENING PATH OF THE LABYRINTH?

CHAPTER 3

HOW TO WALK A LABYRINTH

INTRODUCTION AND PERFORMANCE OBJECTIVES

The success of most human endeavors depends on how one prepares to accomplish it. This is especially true when it comes to walking the labyrinth. This chapter provides simple instructions on how to prepare for and walk a labyrinth.

Although everyone's reaction to walking a labyrinth is different, most people agree that the walk connects us to the Earth. Feeling the ground under our feet, hearing the sounds of nature and walking a similar path that others have walked over the centuries, create a powerful connection with the human family, the wonders of Earth's creation and the universe.

At the conclusion of this chapter, students will:

- walk the labyrinth using the three Rs: relaxing, receiving and returning.

- become aware of caring for the Earth through readings about Chief Seattle, Earth Day, Al Gore and the Earth Charter.

- place the concept of the Earth within the total universe.

- learn to respect the earth through math, poetry, art and music.

PREPARATION FOR THE LABYRINTH WALK

There is no right or wrong way to walk a labyrinth. However, some suggestions may be helpful to enhance the experience.

- Approach the labyrinth with respect and openness.

- Quiet yourself as you prepare for the walk.

- Be aware of sights and sounds around you.

- Push away any worries, concerns or distractions.

- Know beforehand that you will pass others coming and going on the path; simply step aside to let them pass.

- Remove your shoes, unless walking on an in-ground labyrinth or shoes are needed for support.

THE THREE Rs

An excellent guide on how to walk the labyrinth is to think of the three Rs: relaxing, receiving and returning. Relaxing is associated with entering the labyrinth, receiving is associated with the center of the labyrinth and returning is associated with the walk out of the labyrinth.

RELAXING (ENTERING THE LABYRINTH)

- Pause at the entrance to the labyrinth.
- Breathe deeply.
- When ready, enter and walk at your own pace.
- Feel the floor or ground beneath your feet.
- Be aware of your feelings as you walk.

RECEIVING (CENTER OF THE LABYRINTH)

- Be still.
- Take the time to feel what it is like to be at the center.
- Be aware of any words or feelings that surface in you.
- Stay at the center as long as you wish; leave when you are ready.

RETURNING (WALKING OUT OF THE LABYRINTH)

- Follow the same path out; the path out is the same as the way in.
- Select one word or feeling you received at the center of the labyrinth that needs your attention.
- Decide how you can integrate the feeling or word in your daily life.
- When finished, turn toward the center and nod your head as an expression of thanks for the experience.

AFTER THE WALK

- Sit quietly outside the labyrinth.
- Share your experience with others, if you wish.
- Write, draw or paint what your experience was like.

THE LABYRINTH, ONE WITH THE EARTH AND THE HUMAN FAMILY

Pioneers concerned for the Earth are found throughout history. Three particular people and one special document come to mind in our own century. The people are Chief Seattle, Senator Gaylord Nelson and former Vice President, Al Gore. The important document that affects global awareness for a sustainable future is the Earth Charter.

CHIEF SEATTLE'S LETTER

Native Americans had a profound awareness of the unity between the land and its people. Chief Seattle's famous line, "The earth does not belong to man, man belongs to the Earth", is often quoted.

In 1852, the U. S. Government under Franklin Pierce inquired about purchasing land from Chief Seattle's tribe. Chief Seattle wrote this marvelous letter in reply.

"The President in Washington sends word that he wishes to buy our land. But how can you buy or sell the sky? The land? The idea is strange to us. If we do not own the freshness of the air and the sparkle of the water, how can you buy them?

Every part of the earth is sacred to my people: every shining pine needle, every sandy shore, every mist in the dark woods, every meadow, every humming insect. All are holy in the memory and experience of my people.

We know the sap which courses through the trees as we know the blood that courses through our veins. We are part of the earth and it is part of us. The perfumed flowers are our sisters. The bear, the deer, the great eagle, these are our brothers. The rocky crests, the dew in the meadow, the body heat of the pony and man all belong to the same family.

The rivers are our brothers. They quench our thirst. They carry our canoes and feed our children. So you must give the rivers the kindness that you would give any brother.

If we sell you our land, remember that the air is precious to us, that the air shares its spirit with all the life that it supports. The wind that gave our grandfather his first breath also received his last sigh. The wind also gives our children the spirit of life. So if we sell our land, you must keep it apart and sacred, as a place where man can go to taste the wind that is sweetened by the meadow flowers.

Will you teach your children that the earth is our mother? What befalls the earth befalls all the sons of the earth.

This we know: the earth does not belong to man, man belongs to the earth. All things are connected like the blood that unites us all. Man did not weave the web of life; he is merely a strand in it. Whatever he does to the web, he does to himself.

One thing we know: our God is also your God. The earth is precious to him and to harm the earth is to heap contempt on its creator.

Your destiny is a mystery to us. What will happen when the buffalo are all slaughtered? The wild horses tamed? What will happen when the secret corners of the forest are heavy with the scent of many men and the view of the ripe hills is blotted with talking wires? Where will the thicket be? Gone! Where will the eagle be? Gone! And what is left to say goodbye to the swift pony and then the hunt? The end of living and the beginning of survival!

When the last Red man has vanished with the wilderness and his memory is only the shadow of a cloud moving across the prairie, will these shores and forests still be here? Will there be any of the spirit of my people left?

We love this earth as a newborn loves its mother's heartbeat. So, if we sell you our land, love it as we have loved it. Care for it as we have cared for it. Hold in your mind the memory of the land as it is when you receive it. Preserve the land for all children and love it as God loves us.

As we are part of the land, you too are part of the land. This earth is precious to us. It is also precious to you.

One thing we know — there is only one God. No man, be he Red man or White man, can be apart. We are all brothers after all."

SENATOR GAYLORD NELSON – FOUNDER OF EARTH DAY

In 1962, Gaylord Nelson was elected to the Senate and began an 18 year career in Congress. He sought ways to focus public attention on the environment, declaring, "We cannot be blind to the growing crisis of our environment. Our soil, our water, and our air are becoming more polluted every day. Our most priceless natural resources—trees, lakes, rivers, wildlife habitats, scenic landscapes—are being destroyed."

His greatest achievement was as Founder of Earth Day. How did the first Earth day come about? Here is the story in Senator Nelson's own words.

"Actually, the idea for Earth Day evolved over a period of seven years starting in 1962. For several years, it had been troubling me that the state of our environment was simply a non-issue in the politics of the country. Finally, in November of 1962, an idea occurred to me that was, I thought, a virtual cinch to put the environment into the political "limelight" once and for all. The idea was to persuade President Kennedy to give visibility to this issue by going on a national conservation tour. I flew to Washington to discuss the proposal with Attorney General Robert Kennedy, who liked the idea. So did the President. The President began his five-day, eleven-state conservation tour in September, 1963. For many reasons the tour did not succeed in putting the issue onto the national political agenda. However, it was the germ of the idea that ultimately flowered into Earth Day.

I continued to speak on environmental issues to a variety of audiences in some twenty-five states. All across the country, evidence of environmental degradation was appearing everywhere and everyone noticed except the political establishment. The environmental issue simply was not to be found on the nation's political agenda. The people were concerned but the politicians were not.

After President Kennedy's tour, I still hoped for some idea that would thrust the environment into the political mainstream. Six years would pass before the idea that became Earth Day would occur to me while on a conservation speaking tour out West in the summer of 1969. At the time, the Vietnam War demonstrations occurred on campuses all across the nation. Suddenly, the idea occurred to me - why not organize a huge grassroots protest over what was happening to our environment.

I was satisfied that if we could tap into the environmental concerns of the general public and infuse the student anti-war energy into the environmental cause, we could generate a demonstration that would force this issue onto the political agenda. It was a big gamble, but worth a try.

At a conference in Seattle in September, 1969, I announced that in the spring of 1970, there would be a nationwide grassroots demonstration on behalf of the environment and invited everyone to participate. The wire services carried the story from coast to coast. The response was electric. It took off like gangbusters. Telegrams, letters and telephone inquiries poured in from all across the country. The American people finally had a forum to express their concerns about what was happening to the land, rivers, lakes and air- and they did so with spectacular exuberance. For the next four months, two members of my Senate staff, Linda Billings and John Herage, managed Earth Day affairs out of my Senate office.

Five months before Earth Day, on Sunday, November 30, 1969, *The New York Times* carried a lengthy article by Galdwin Hill reporting on the astonishing proliferation of environmental events: "Rising concern about the environmental crisis is sweeping the nation's campuses with an intensity that may be on its way to eclipsing student discontent over the war in Vietnam...a national day of observance of environmental problems...is being planned for next spring...when a nationwide environmental "teach-in"...coordinated from the office of Senator Gaylord Nelson is planned..."

It was obvious that we were headed for a spectacular success on Earth Day. It was also obvious that grassroots activities had ballooned beyond the capacity of U.S. Senate office staff to keep up with the telephone calls, paper work, inquiries, etc. In mid-January, three months before Earth Day, John Gardner, Founder of Common Cause, provided temporary space for a Washington, D.C. headquarters. I staffed the office with college students and selected Denis Hayes as coordinator of activities.

Earth Day worked because of the spontaneous response at the grassroots level. We had neither the time nor resources to organize 20 million demonstrators and the thousands of schools and local communities that participated. That was the remarkable thing about Earth Day. It organized itself." (From the Wilderness Society)

VICE PRESIDENT AL GORE, AN INCONVENIENT TRUTH

Former Vice President Al Gore is another environmentalist. Gore makes protecting the environment a focus of his public career, educating Congress and the public on the dangers of global warming. His film, *An Inconvenient Truth*, won an Oscar for best documentary in 2006. The paperback book of the same title topped the New York Times best-seller list for nonfiction.

Though some are critical of his book and film, what Gore did was to emphasize the need for change on an international level. He traveled and showed the film more than 1,000 times across the world, believing every nation was affected by global warming and every nation must be part of its solution.

He continues to make critical contributions on the subject in a sequel book, *A Path to Survival*. The text is a visionary blueprint for the changes that should be made as a world community. The book, according to an Associated Press release, is described as, "Part scientific manual, part expose and a visionary call for a new planet-wide political movement. The book will appeal to those who were motivated by the call to action of *An Inconvenient Truth* and for those who are now ready to fight for the solutions that were considered politically impossible only a short time ago." Throughout his career, Gore has made and continues to make critical contributions to the protection of the environment. His work earned him the Nobel Peace Prize in 2007.

THE EARTH CHARTER

In 1987, the United Nations Commission on the Environment and Development issued a call for a new charter setting forth principles for a sustainable future for our world. The drafting of the charter was the unfinished business of the Rio de Janeiro Earth Summit in 1992. The process took ten years of consultation with thousands of individuals, experts, grass root communities and organizations from all over the world. The Earth Commission circulated the draft internationally as part of the consultation process. The commission approved the draft in March of 2000 and the official launching of the charter occurred on June 29, 2000 in the Peace Palace at the Hague. A short outline of the charter's mission statement and principles are included in this chapter.

From the previous readings on environmental pioneers and the Earth Charter, two movements toward environmental growth surfaced. The first is that the life of our Earth is in critical condition. The second is that solutions to the problem must be global. The world is now a universal family. As Chief Seattle stated, "All things are connected like the blood that unites us all." Whatever we do to the Earth, one way or another, we do to ourselves.

AN EARTH CHARTER OUTLINE

MISSION

DECLARATION OF FUNDAMENTAL PRINCIPLES FOR BULDING A JUST, SUSTAINABLE AND PEACEFUL GLOBAL SOCIETY IN THE 21ST CENTURY.

It requires global interdependence and shared responsibility for the human family in the larger world.

It expresses hope and a call to help create a global partnership at a critical juncture in history.

PRINCIPLES

Respect and Care for the Community of Life

Recognize all beings are interdependent. With the right of ownership comes the duty to prevent environmental harm. Guarantee human rights for all to reach one's full potential. Transmit values, traditions and institutions to future generations.

Ecological Integrity

Manage the use of renewable resources: water, soil, forests and marine life. Prevent pollution of any part of the environment. Reduce, reuse and recycle materials used in production. Adopt life styles that stress quality of life and material sufficiency.

Social and Economic Justice

Promote equitable distribution of wealth within and among nations. Secure human rights of women and girls and end all violence against them. Eliminate discrimination in all forms. Protect and restore outstanding places of cultural and spiritual value.

Democracy, Non-violence and Peace

Eliminate corruption in all public and private institutions. Promote the arts, humanities and science in sustainable education. Eliminate nuclear, biological and toxic weapons and other weapons of mass destruction. Recognize peace is created by right relationships with oneself, other persons, cultures and other life.

ACADEMIC INTEGRATION
SCIENCE/MATH - ONE WITH THE UNIVERSE

"Scientists say that we are one with the universe. We are made of the same stardust. It all began twenty billion (20,000,000,000) years ago. A tiny speck of light, no bigger than a pin prick, lived alone in total darkness. There came a split second when the tiny speck bursting with energy became a primeval fireball, often referred to as the Big Bang. The fire ball was the size of a grapefruit that held within itself all that is, was and ever will be.

During the next five billion years, the fireball grew to become the universe. The universe holds one trillion (1,000,000,000,000) galaxies. Within each galaxy, there are a hundred billion (100,000,000,000) stars.

Two billion years after the universe came into being, a group of stars in one of the galaxies, the Milky Way, died or went to supernova. These stars left billions of bits of themselves behind and became the solar system. The solar system includes the sun and planets that revolve around the sun. One of these planets is Earth.

Earth is the third planet from the sun.

The Earth is between Venus and Mars.

The Earth has one moon.

Earth is larger than Pluto, Mercury, Venus and Mars.

Earth is smaller than Jupiter, Saturn, Uranus and Neptune.

The distance around the Earth is 7,926.2 miles.

The Earth turns on its axis every 23 hours, 56 minutes and 4 seconds.

It takes the Earth 365.2 days to go around the sun.

The creation story is not finished. What humans do on the Earth either continues to create or destroy it. The preservation of the world depends on what each individual does in his or her small space on the planet. We are one with the universe as co-creators."   Sally Marsh

MATH - THE DECIMAL SYSTEM

The Big Bang occurred over 13 million years ago. When reading huge numbers about the universe, they tend to boggle the mind. The decimal system is a way of writing numbers, from huge quantities to tiny fractions, using only ten basic symbols: 1, 2, 3, 4, 5, 6, 7, 8, 9, 0. It was developed by Hindu mathematicians in India more than 2,000 years ago.

The value of a number depends on where the number is located. The number 2 alone has a different value than the 2 in the number 246 or 823. The value of each place, call a digit, is ten times greater than the value of the number placed just to its right. Study the Place Value Grid.

1,000,000	Millions		.1	1/10	Tenths
100,000	Hundred Thousands		.01	1/100	Hundredths
10,000	Ten Thousands		.001	1/1,000	Thousandths
1,000	One Thousands		.0001	1/10,000	Ten Thousandths
100	One Hundreds		.00001	1/100,000	Hundred Thousandths
10	Tens				
1	Ones				

Although the grid includes numbers less than one to the right of the decimal point, the concern here is only the whole numbers left of the decimal point. When words like two million are used, they are easy to read. Using the figures, 2,000,000, requires a bit of thinking. How many zeros are needed to make a million? A billion? A trillion? Reading or writing a number like 8,624,847,002,070 needs even more thought.

Another way to simplify the reading or writing of numbers is to separate three numbers with a comma, from right to left, beginning with hundreds.

8,	624,	847,	002,	070
trillion,	billion	**million,**	**thousands,**	hundreds

The number is read as: eight *trillion*, six hundred twenty four billion, eight hundred forty seven **million**, two **thousand**, seventy.

Use the place value grid to write these written words into numbers.

1. The Andromeda galaxies are over <u>two million</u> light years away. _____

2. The birth of the universe was over <u>thirteen billion</u> years ago. _____

3. The sun is about <u>ninety three million</u> miles from the Earth. _____

4 The birth of our solar system occurred about <u>five billion</u> years ago. _____

5. The speed of light is about <u>one hundred eighty six thousand</u> miles per second. _____

6. Some galaxies rotate at a speed of <u>sixty thousand</u> miles per second. _____

7. The diameter of Mars is <u>four thousand, two hundred and thirteen</u> miles. _____

8. The diameter of the Earth is about <u>seven thousand, nine hundred, twenty six</u> miles. _____

9. The Milky Way Galaxy contains <u>a trillion</u> times the mass of the sun. _____

10. The moon is <u>two hundred forty thousand</u> miles away from the Earth. _____

SCIENTIFIC NOTATION

Scientists often deal with very large numbers. They use the power of 10 to write large numbers in a shorthand method called scientific notation, which uses a small number times a power of ten.

$90,000,000 = 9 \times 10,000,000 = 9 \times 10^7$ (90 million)

$3,000,000,000 = 3 \times 10^9$ (3 billion)

$4,000,000 = 4 \times 10^6$ (4 million)

$8,000 = 8 \times 10^3$ (8 thousand)

Fill in the blanks.

10	$=$	1	10^3	$=$	$1,000$	$10^6 =$	_____
10	$=$	10	10^4	$=$	$10,000$	$10^7 =$	_____
10	$=$	100	10^5	$=$	_____	$10^8 =$	_____

Find the value of these scientific notations.

SCIENTIFIC NOTATION		VALUE	SCIENTIFIC NOTATION		VALUE
5×10^2	$=$	_____	9×10^7	$=$	_____
7×10^8	$=$	_____	2×10^5	$=$	_____

Fill in the lines.

_____ x 10_ = 4,000   _____ x 10   = 8,000

_____ x 10_ = 60,000   _____ x 1000 = 4,000

_____ x 10_ = 2,000,000

_____ x 10_ = 800,000,000

EARTH MUSIC – ONE

What follows is an abridged song that could be recited rhythmically with alternating voices.

One with the Buffalo	One with the Bear
One with the Meadow	One with the Mare
One with the Redwood	One with the Rock
One with the Eagle	One with the Hawk
One with the Blue Sky	One with the Storm
One with the Winter	One with the Warm
One with the Thunder	One with the Rain
One with the Laughter	One with the Pain
One with the Shadow	One with the Light
One with the Sunrise	One with the Night
One with the Sorrow	One with the Joy
One with the Fullness	One with the Void
One with the Sparrow	One with the Song
One with the Righteous	One with the Wrong
One with the Morning	One with the Dew
One with the Mountains	One with the View
One with the Seeker	One with the Sought
One with the Teacher	One with the Taught
One with the Trinket	One with the Jewel

One with the Master

One with the Shining

One with the Knowing

One with the Music

One with the Branches

One with the Meaning

One with the Part

One with the Dying

One with the Other

One with the Fool

One with the Star

One with the Why

One with the Flute

One with the Root

One with the Word

One with the Whole

One with the Life

One with the One

ONE WITH ALL BEINGS UNDER THE SUN.

HL0021000

Earth Family

Jan Novotka

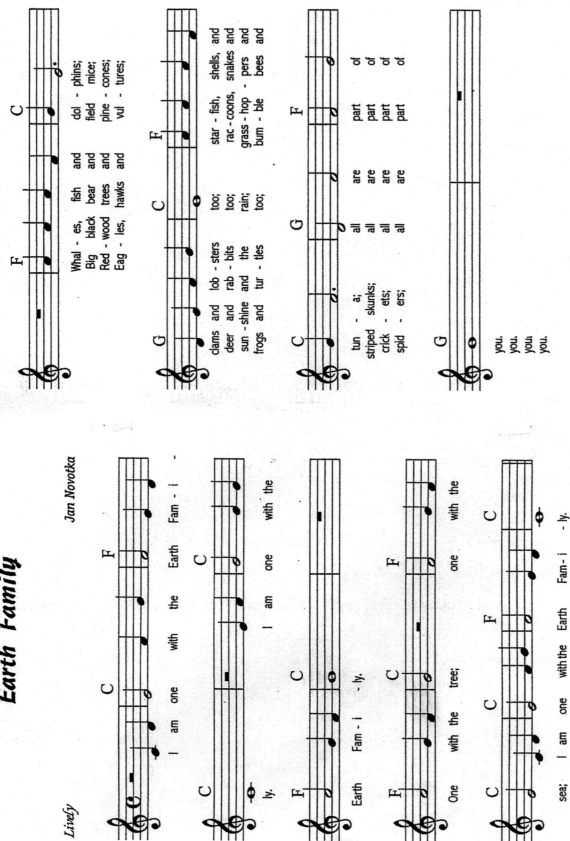

ART — EARTH SPHERE

MATERIALS

Acrylic craft paint — three or four colors.

Clear acrylic ornaments.

Colorful cording, ribbon.

Alcohol.

Elmer's Glue.

INSTRUCTIONS

1. Remove hanger, cap, or top from ornament.

2. Rinse inside of ornament with alcohol.

3. Dry thoroughly.

4. Squeeze a small amount of the first paint color inside of the ornament so that it runs down the side.

5. Rotate ornament until there are three or four lines of paint.

6. Add next color between places of the first color.

7. Add one or two more colors in the same way.

8. Rest ornament on its side for five minutes.

9. Rotate a quarter turn every five to ten minutes until paint covers all of the inside.

10. Pour out excess paint.

11. Continue to rotate over the next DAY to coat the ornament evenly. Colors will continue to move and change with each turn.

12. When the desired effect is achieved, drain excess paint from the inside of ornament.

THE PAINT IN THE ORNAMENT WILL TAKE FOUR TO FIVE DAYS TO DRY COMPLETELY.

13. Use Elmer's glue to paste the top of the ornament where the hanger fits.

14. Use a colorful ribbon or cord with a small knot or bow to hang the sphere.

ECOLOGY LABYRINTH WALK

The word ecology comes from Greek and means house. The theme of this labyrinth walk is to consider the Earth as home. The Earth is not owned or rented by anyone. It is loaned to its inhabitants who consist of one household, all of whom are responsible to care for the Earth indefinitely. Housemates in this home are required to follow three basic rules:

1. Use only your share of the goods.

2. Clean up after yourself.

3. Keep the house in good condition.

Process

- At the center of the labyrinth, place an Earth Ball.

- Review the three Rs on how to walk the labyrinth.

- Suggest a few ways to be friendlier toward the Earth and what people can do to care for their small piece of Earth so others may have a future.

- As each person leaves the labyrinth, he or she is given a copy of the Earth Charter.
  (To obtain copies, go to http://www.earthcharter.org.)

LABYRINTH WALK FOLLOW-UP ACTIVITY

Study ways to save the Earth and the environment. Make your own chart similar to the sample given and check off activities accomplished.

WAYS TO SAVE THE EARTH

Here are a few suggestions on how to help save the environment.

- Use recycled paper.

- Turn off the TV when you finish watching it.

- Feed the birds or put up a bird house.

- Use both sides of a sheet of paper.

- Help recycle paper, cans, glass and plastic.

- Shut off water while brushing your teeth.

- Pick up and throw litter in the trash can.

- When possible, ride your bike or walk to lessen pollution from cars.

- Turn off lights when leaving a room.

- Wash vegetables and fruits before eating them.

- Use sponges or washable cloths instead of paper towels.

- Get what you want out of the refrigerator and quickly close the door.

- Try not to buy plastic.

- Use only the necessary amount of water for a cup of cocoa, tea, etc.

- Use cold water for laundry.

- Reuse scrap paper.

- Write the word Earth with a capital letter to give it importance.

- Plant flowers and trees.

Use the sample chart below to list the activities you can do to help with the environment

	MON.	TUES.	WED.	THURS.	FRI.
RECYCLE PAPER					
WRITE ON BOTH SIDES OF THE PAPER					
SAVE UNWANTED PAPER, CANS, BOTTLES, PLASTICS					
PUT LITTER IN TRASH CANS					
TURN OFF LIGHTS WHEN LEAVING THE ROOM					
PLANT FLOWERS AND TREES					
PICK UP PAPERS AND TRASH					
OTHER					

PROJECT: If there is a labyrinth within your area that requires maintenance, volunteer to help.

CHAPTER 4

LABYRINTH AND MAZE DESIGNS

INTRODUCTION AND PERFORMANCE OBJECTIVES

Many people today confuse the labyrinth with the maze. The purpose of this chapter is to point out their differences and show illustrations of both designs. Additional hands-on activities with mazes and labyrinths help clarify the distinction between the two.

Directions are provided on how to draw labyrinths from the seed pattern in order to enable students to understand more fully its basic structure. Also included is a brief explanation of the functions of the left-and-right-sides of the brain and why walking the labyrinth is considered a right-brain activity.

Because the labyrinth is sometimes used to solve problems, this chapter concludes with six simple problem-solving steps and how to apply them to implementing a labyrinth walk metaphor.

Upon completion of this chapter, students will:

- become aware of the various types and designs of labyrinths and mazes.

- clarify the distinction between labyrinths and mazes.

- draw various labyrinth designs from their seed patterns.

- understand why the labyrinth walk is considered a right-brain activity.

- learn problem-solving techniques when implementing a labyrinth metaphor.

THE DISTINCTION BETWEEN A LABYRINTH AND A MAZE

Perhaps one of the reasons why the labyrinth and maze is confused is that Webster's dictionary has the same meaning for both words. Because the definitions are used interchangeably, it makes their unique difference blurred. For example, the word <u>labyrinth</u> in the dictionary is defined in two ways as:

1. An intricate combination of paths or passages in which it is difficult to find one's way or to reach an exit.

2. A maze of paths bordered by high hedges, as in a park or garden.

Webster's definition of a labyrinth describes a <u>maze</u>. The dictionary provides an illustration of a maze but labels it a labyrinth.

LABYRINTH  MAZE

The definition of a <u>maze</u> is listed as:

A confusing network of paths or passages; labyrinth.

In actuality, the labyrinth and the maze are two distinct paths, walked for entirely different reasons. A maze is a puzzle with many paths that lead to an exit. Some paths are false, others are dead ends. Because there are so many choices on which path to follow, one can easily get lost in a maze. The purpose of walking a maze is to solve a puzzle.

In contrast, a labyrinth has one winding path that leads to a center and back out again on the same path. One cannot get lost in a labyrinth. The purpose of walking a labyrinth varies: relaxation, peace, fun, meditation, special-day celebrations or solving problems.

To qualify as a maze, a design must have choices in the pathway.

To qualify as a labyrinth, a design should have one path.

THE LABYRINTH DESIGN

The physical representation of the labyrinth design survived through centuries of history, although the actual dating of these designs is uncertain. Historically, the oldest reliable design came from Southern Europe where different designs surfaced.

THE CRETAN LABYRINTH

This design was found on Cretan coins over 4,000 years ago. It is one of the most popular labyrinth designs used today.

THE ROMAN LABYRINTH

The Roman design, found mainly on floor mosaics, was discovered around the year 324 in Algeria. The design has four quadrants.

THE MEDIEVAL LABYRINTH

This design was used mainly as a manuscript illustration dating back to the 9th century. The design is a forerunner of the labyrinth found three centuries later at Chartres Cathedral in France.

THE CHARTRES LABYRINTH

The Chartres Labyrinth is the best known design. Its unique decorative lines add to its popularity. Like the Cretan labyrinth, it is used all over the world.

OTHER CREATIVE DESIGNS OVER THE CENTURIES

MODERN DAY LABYRINTH DESIGNS

The reasons the labyrinth design endured over such a long period of time are difficult to determine. Perhaps it was because the symbol is associated with good fortune, protection, insight, oneness, and connectedness to nature or universal appeal. What is certain, however, is that the labyrinth is experiencing a revival in modern day society, particularly the Cretan and Chartres designs.

LABYRINTH CIRCUITS

Although labyrinths are identified by name, such as Roman, Cretan, etc. they are often referred to by the number of CIRCUITS they contain. Labyrinths may have 3, 4, 5, 7, 11, 13 or 15 circuits. The most common numbers are the 7-circuit labyrinth and the 11-circuit labyrinth.

SEVEN CIRCUIT

CIRCUIT

ELEVEN CIRCUIT

Today, labyrinth designs range from highly artistic configurations to simple lines in the sand. They are found in hospitals, schools, businesses, prisons, churches, retreat centers, and recreational parks, to name but a few.

THE MAZE DESIGN

According to *National Geographic Magazine*, "Many different types and classifications of mazes are found all over the world today. One of the most popular mazes is found at Dole Pineapple Plantation in Hawaii. The Guiness Book of Records, 2001, recognizes this maze, the Pineapple Garden Maze, as the largest in the world. It covers two acres, its path is 1.7 miles long and it is made of 11,400 colorful Hawaiian plants. Notice the pineapple in its center.

Everywhere you look you see plants towering high above your head. You turn in circles trying to remember where you've been and to guess which way you should go. You decide to race down an open tunnel, only to find that you can't make your way through the dense plants. Where are you? A jungle? No, you're in the middle of a hedge maze, trying to find the exit.

Mazes have been around for at least 4,000 years. Early mazes, however, were very different from today's mazes. They were called labyrinths. In a labyrinth, there is only one continuous pathway to reach the goal. For a long time some groups, such as the ancient Egyptians, used these mazes for rituals.

It wasn't until about a thousand years ago that mazes became the fun puzzles that we have today. In the 17th century, English kings and queens began to use mazes called hedge mazes as amusement parks. In these mazes, tall hedges prevent visitors from seeing the exit. Still popular today, many hedge mazes are found around the world. Some are even made from cornstalks."

From the history of the labyrinth and maze, it is understandable how the two got confused. Modern designers know the labyrinth is not a maze, nor is a maze a labyrinth. (http://nationalgeographic.com/ngkids/0108/maze/)

PENCIL-WALKING LABYRINTHS AND MAZES

In the illustrations that follow, use a pencil to move toward the center of the labyrinth and back out again and solve maze puzzles from start to finish.

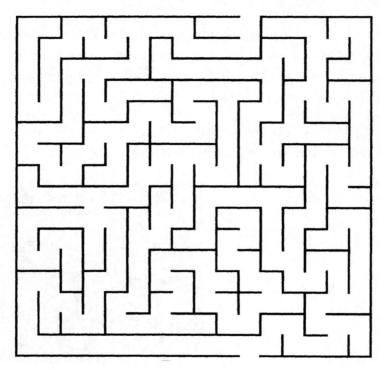

PENCIL-WALKING LABYRINTHS AND MAZES continued.

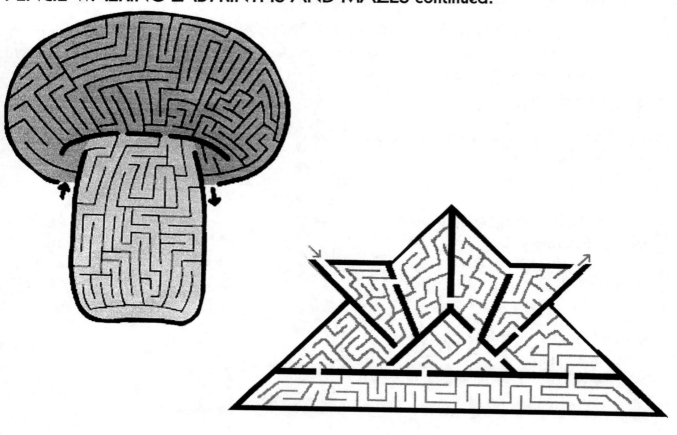

DRAWING THE THREE-CIRCUIT LABYRINTH FROM THE SEED PATTERN

Drawing the design for the labyrinth begins with the SEED PATTERN. The pattern differs depending on the number of circuits in the labyrinth. Obviously, the three-circuit labyrinth is the easiest. Study these directions on how to draw a three-circuit labyrinth.

THE SEED PATTERN

1. Start with a cross and a dot in each of the four sections as shown in the picture.

2. Connect the top line of the cross with the top right dot. Form a loop.

3. Connect the top left dot with the right hand cross. Form a loop.

4. Connect the left line of the cross with the right side bottom dot.

5. Connect the bottom left dot to the line on the bottom of the cross.

DRAWING THE SEVEN-CIRCUIT LABYRINTH FROM THE SEED PATTERN

Below is a step-by-step illustration on how to draw a seven-circuit labyrinth from the seed pattern to its completion. The basic process is to connect dots and lines from left to right using broad strokes.

1. Draw a cross.	2. Add right angles on left and right, top and bottom.
3. Add four dots on the left and right, top and bottom angles. This forms the basic SEED PATTERN.	4. Connect the top line of cross with top right angle, making an arch.
5. Make an arch by connecting the vertical top of the left angle with the top right dot.	6. Make an arch by connecting the top left dot with the horizontal line at the top right angle.

7. Make an arch by connecting the horizontal line on the top left angle with the right horizontal line on the cross.

8. Make an arch by connecting the left horizontal line of the cross with the horizontal line on the lower right angle.

9. Make an arch by connecting the horizontal line of the bottom left angle with the lower left dot.

10. Connect bottom left dot to the vertical line on the bottom right angle, making an arch.

11. Connect the vertical line of the bottom left angle to the vertical line of the cross.

SEED PATTERN ACTIVITY

The best way to understand the design of a labyrinth is to draw one from the seed patterns. To do so utilizes both sides of the brain; the analytical-left side and the intuitive-right side. Draw it over and over again until the hand can do it without the directions or pictures of each step.

On a separate piece of paper, place these patterns on the lower half of the paper to provide enough space to build the path upward. Make the spaces between each loop the same distance.

Try to figure out the third seed pattern. What number of circuits is in this pattern?

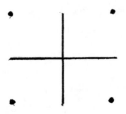

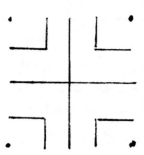

COMPUTER RESEARCH

Consult Karen's Labyrinth Page on the computer and draw an eleven-circuit seed pattern from her instructions.

BIOLOGY – THE BRAIN
WALKING THE LABYRINTH, A RIGHT-BRAIN ACTIVITY

Walking the labyrinth is said to be a right-brain activity. What does this mean?

The brain in the human skull is the organ that controls the body's movement and intellectual activities. It continually receives information from the senses about things that happen outside and inside the body. Although there are many parts to the brain, three main parts are mentioned here:

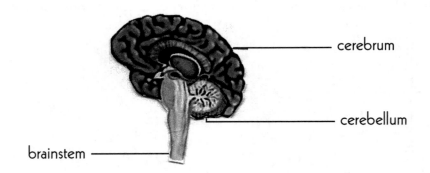

1. brainstem	The brainstem is in charge of all important body functions needed to stay alive: breathing, digesting food and circulating blood. It also controls muscles that move automatically, on their own. The brainstem has two halves, one on the right side and one on the left side.
2. cerebrum	This is the biggest part of the brain and makes up 85% of the brain's weight. The memory lives here and controls voluntary muscles. It is the center of thinking, making learning and remembering possible.
3. cerebellum	This part maintains the body's balance, posture and body movements. It is 1/8 of the brain size.

Before the beginning of the 20th century, little was known of the brain. In the 50's and 60's, research was done by Roger Sperry which earned him the Nobel Prize in Medicine in 1981. He maintained that the brain is divided into two hemispheres, the right brain and the left brain. Although both sides of the brain are involved in every human activity, each hemisphere has its own style of thinking and learning ability. One side is more dominant (controlling) than the other. Consider these differences between the left and right side of the brain.

LEFT SIDE OF THE BRAIN	RIGHT SIDE OF THE BRAIN
Verbal (pertaining to words)	Non-verbal
Linear (arranged in a line)	Uses imagination (forms a mental picture of things not present)

LEFT SIDE OF THE BRAIN	RIGHT SIDE OF THE BRAIN
Sequential (place things in logical order)	Creative (forms a new thought, idea or thing)
Precise (knows from exact reasoning)	Intuitive (knows by feeling, not from reasoning)
Rational (based on reason)	Emotional (based on feelings)
Objective (not influenced by feelings)	Subjective (influenced by personal feelings)
Looks at the parts	Looks at the whole
Problem solver	Spontaneous actions without effort

No one person is totally left brained or right brained. One side may be more dominant than the other. Just as there is a dominant eye, foot or hand, there is a dominant side of the brain. Although it is natural and more comfortable to use the stronger, dominant side over the other, both sides of the brain should be developed and used. A balanced brain makes a balanced person.

LEFT-SIDE, RIGHT-SIDE BRAIN ACTIVITY.

Is your left or right brain more dominant? Here are some questions to help you decide.

1. When you walk in a room, do you prefer the left or right side?

2. When taking a test, do you like multiple choice (objective, subjective or discussion)?

3. Do you often have hunches or gut-level feelings?

4. Do you have a place for everything and everything in its place?

5. Do you do things in a planned, orderly way?

6. Do you like verbal (word) instructions rather than visual pictures?

7. When assembling things, do you read the directions first?

8. Is it easier to remember people's names or faces?

9. When someone is talking, do you respond to the person's words or feelings?

10. Do you solve a problem without knowing if the answer is correct?

How might walking a labyrinth help the functions of your brain?

PROBLEM SOLVING TO IMPLEMENT THE LABYRINTH METAPHOR

Chapter two introduced the meaning of a metaphor, stating that it was a word or group of words that compared two unlike objects or ideas. The chapter also explained that the labyrinth was a metaphor for life's journey. What this statement means is that the metaphor or message received during a labyrinth walk is compared to something that happened or is happening in one's life. Because the mind and body are relaxed during the walk, a metaphor or message may surface. The metaphor basically tells us that something recalled from the past or felt in the present moment needs attention.

The metaphor may range from simple enjoyment, peace, relaxation to more complex issues. The implementation of some metaphors is easily resolved during or returning from the center of the labyrinth walk. Other metaphors many require more thought and time.

Remember that the labyrinth is also a tool for transformation and change. Therefore, implementing the metaphor as a follow-up to the labyrinth walk is helpful for transformation or change to occur. Some metaphors may require more problem solving techniques to foster positive change.

What follows is a six-step process that might be helpful when implementing a more complex metaphor. The example given in this chapter is a further development of the metaphor written in chapter two where John failed to pass his science GED test.

1. Identify the Metaphor.

2. Analyze the Metaphor.

3. Brainstorm Ways to Implement the Metaphor.

4. Select One Method of Implementation.

5. Implement the Metaphor.

6. Evaluate the Process.

1. IDENTIFY THE METAPHOR

Obviously, to identify the metaphor one must know what it is. To do this, simply ask questions like: What is attracting my attention at this moment? What message is my body giving me? What is the issue that has the most concern? Give a name to the experience. In John's case it was a failed science exam that prevented him from getting his GED.

2. ANALYZE THE METAPHOR

To analyze the metaphor is to go beyond the surface identity and give it deeper meaning. This step of the process deals with feelings that accompany the metaphor and how they affect the person walking. At this stage, one seeks inner wisdom from the body about the situation and why it may have occurred.

John asked himself some important questions. If he could pass other parts of the GED test, why did he fail science? What were his study habits? Did he spend more time studying for one test over another? What else was happening in his life that may have contributed to the failure? What were the consequences if he failed again?

John's predominant feeling during the walk was one of sadness because he didn't pass. John knew that success in life was hindered without a GED. His teacher was also disappointed in him. When considering these points, John concluded the reason he failed was the presumption that he didn't need to study as much because he was a good student and could wing it. In addition, science was his least favorite subject and he didn't want to put time into studying it. Analyzing made the situation a lot clearer.

3. BRAINSTORM WAYS TO IMPLEMENT THE METAPHOR

What needs to be done at this point of the process is to consider ways to transform or change the situation or behavior. To address the brainstorming phase, create a list of possibilities and alternative ways to act. Think creatively. The most unexpected thought may be worth considering. Seek additional information needed to make a good decision. If necessary, assistance can be obtained from others: advisors, counselors, mentors or others important in one's life.

Some possibilities and alternatives that John might consider are:

• Go back to a regular high school where he can study science over a longer period of time.

• Study harder to pass the GED science component.

• Get tutored in science.

• Ask the GED teacher for additional help.

• Forget the whole thing and get a job instead.

• Get training in another trade.

• Earn a license to drive a truck, bus or taxi.

4. SELECT ONE METHOD OF IMPLEMENTATION

This step is a refining process among many possibilities of alternatives. Look at each possibility and the risks or advantages involved. Ask how the decision would affect other people in your life. Can you finance your choice? What is your heart really telling you? Do you want to take the test again or move on to something else? Is what you choose realistic and manageable? Think of the rewards received when the metaphor is implemented successfully. The choice you make depends on many circumstances.

John felt he could pass the science test with additional help and support. His teacher believed he was a good student. After much consideration, John asked his teacher for help and planned to take the science test again.

5. IMPLEMENT THE METAPHOR

Knowing what to do is very different from doing it. The real application of the process happens at this stage; planning the when, where, why and how to implement the metaphor within time limits. This step takes time and effort and it must be specific. Don't worry about success yet, just do it and see what happens.

John consulted his teacher about getting extra help in science. The teacher agreed to work with him on Wednesday afternoons from 2 to 3 p.m. until the next GED test is scheduled.

6. EVALUATE THE PROCESS

The question to ask after the implementation process is, was it successful? Most attempts are successful because the results, one way or another, point to a new direction where the process can start all over again at a different level. Congratulations are in order, reward yourself for trying.

PROBLEM SOLVING ACTIVITY

METAPHOR	Philip walked the labyrinth and felt grateful for the $5,000 his grandfather gave him for his graduation from college. How could he use the money wisely to make his grandfather proud of him?
1. IDENTIFY	
2. ANALYZE	
3. BRAINSTORM	
4. METHOD	
5. IMPLEMENT	
6. EVALUATE	

CHAPTER 5

THE SCIENCE OF SACRED GEOMETRY

INTRODUCTION AND PERFORMANCE OBJECTIVES

Simple common shapes like lines, circles, squares, rectangles, triangles and spirals are found everywhere within the universe. Combined in two, three or other multi-dimensional patterns they reflect rare geometric designs of beauty and wholeness. This mathematical science began in ancient times and continues into the modern age with computer-generated fractals. Many patterns possess deep meaning and messages of sacred knowledge. Artists intentionally use these patterns in their work to raise levels of awareness that create moments of "other worldliness". Designs so inspiring are referred to as Sacred Geometry.

Upon completion of this chapter, students will:

- review and study basic geometric shapes, fractals and Platonic solids.

- foster an awareness and appreciation of the beauty, balance and harmony inherent in all living things.

- have a basic understanding of Sacred Geometry.

- study the geometric shapes in the art of Vincent Van Gogh and the structure of Chartres Cathedral.

THE MEANING OF GEOMETRY

To understand the meaning of sacred geometry, one must first consider the meaning of geometry. It is a branch of math that deals with various shapes and forms like points, lines, angles and curves formed on surfaces and solids. Geometry is a field of knowledge that studies geometric relationships that are combined to form unique designs and structures. This diagram illustrates how basic shapes like a dot, line and circle are formed into a triangle, square, sphere and cube.

Begin with a dot.	●
Form a line from the dot.	●————————————▶

A line forms the circle.		
The circle forms a sphere.		
Lines move equally to form a square.		
Square forms a cube.		
Line moves in three equal positions to form a triangle.		
Triangle forms a pyramid.		

Many of these basic shapes combine to form more elaborate two or three-dimensional designs.

Note that these geometric designs are pleasing to the eye because they have balance, harmony, symmetry and proportion. These geometric characteristics show the relationship of many parts to the whole.

PROPORTION	-	proper relations between parts.
BALANCE	-	equal distribution of parts.
HARMONY	-	orderly arrangement between parts.
SYMMETRY	-	equal arrangement of parts.

Among other common shapes are parallel lines =, arch ∩, rectangle ▬, diamond ◊, diagonal line /, left and right angles, and especially the spiral, to name but a few.

THE SPIRAL OF THE LABYRINTH

The labyrinth is an extension of the spiral shape that winds into a circular path. What is unique about the spiral is that it winds around a point while moving away from that point. Note how lines, dots and arches are used to make this seven-circuit labyrinth. This movement can be seen in automation at **http://www.labyreims.com**.

The spiral design is found in nature: the sky, water, wind, ocean waves, sea shells, and in parts of the human body. The spiral is also clearly outlined in a snail. Other examples of spirals are sunflower centers, stars, crystals, shellfish, cobwebs, church windows, river bends and trees.

Spirals are found in the human body: molecules, strands of DNA, cell division, and the eye's cornea. The human heart is a spiral-shaped muscle that pumps blood through many blood vessels. The cochlea too is a spiral-shaped muscle in the inner ear that helps balance the body.

COCHLEA

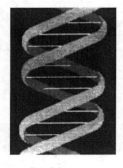
DNA

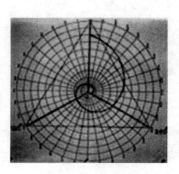
SPIRAL DIAGRAM

The eye of a hurricane and a tornado is a spiral where the wind moves in a counterclockwise direction. Because the eye of a hurricane is large in diameter, the wind appears calmer. The eye of a tornado is small and irregular, making the wind speed more difficult to observe.

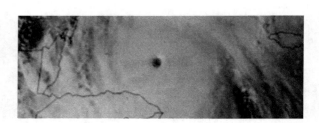

Geographic designs are found in everything within the universe. They are the blueprint of all creation and the architecture of all that is: the circle on the plate on which food is served, the engagement ring on the finger, the face on the clock, the shape of the stars and planets, the lumber from which houses are built, the line of a pencil, the parallel lines in a Venetian blind, the stop sign at the end of the street, the oval shape of the human face and many other examples that could fill a book.

SACRED GEOMETRY

Sacred geometry is an on-going science begun in ancient times and continuing to the present. It is defined in two ways. The first is that geometric forms embody spiritual values within their very nature. Every geometric design has meaning. To the Greeks, the cube symbolized kingship. For example, every structure built for a king would reflect traces of cubic geometry. The five-sided shape of a pentagon is a symbol of fire, earth, air, cosmos and water.

The circle shape depicts heaven or the spirit. The square represents the Earth or matter. To put them together is to square the circle, meaning spirit and matter are united. By studying such designs, one learns about the profound laws of the Universe, thus making these patterns sacred.

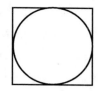

The second meaning comes from the ancient belief concerning the importance of geometry used in religious architecture. Sacred geometry is a universal language that takes ordinary shapes and combines them to create extraordinary structures. It is an expression of beauty that creates moments of AWE. It is a feeling of beauty that one sees, feels, hears and knows, but finds it difficult to put the experience into words.

Music is a mathematical science that is an excellent example that shows the relationship of many parts to the whole. Various rhythms, the arrangement of notes to create harmony, the interweaving of musical themes to tell the story and the different sounds from musical instruments all combine to make a masterpiece of heavenly music.

All one needs to do is listen to the final choral music of Beethoven's *Ninth Symphony* (Ode to Joy) or Handel's Alleluia Chorus from the *Messiah* to know the experience of sacred music. They are so beautiful, they leave one speechless.

FRACTALS

The circle, square and triangle, etc. originated around 300 BCE. However, some designs extend beyond these basic shapes and form more complicated geometric figures called fractals. Fractal geometry is new and research on fractals is happening right now.

Fractals are geometric shapes that are divided into smaller parts where each smaller part is a copy of the whole. This is referred to as self-similarity. The smaller shapes look like the larger original whole. The same appearance is repeated time and time again. Notice the fractal repetition in these ferns.

The word fractal was coined by Benoit Mandelbrot in 1975 and comes from the Latin word meaning broken or fractured. Fractals have existed in the natural world for years. Some examples are found in flowers, trees, water, smoke, lightning, leaves, snowflakes, clouds, mountains, broccoli, pineapple, strawberries, sunflowers and corn.

Within recent years, with the use of a special computer program and math formula, there exists an ability to view fractals with greater depth. Note the difference in these computer-generated designs.

 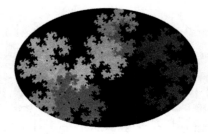

Mandelbrot's theory reveals nature in new ways that cannot be explained in traditional geometric language. The feedback of the math formula fed into the computer is more about quality that expresses infinite detail. Fractals are a complex branch of Sacred Geometry but one that is growing by leaps and bounds. View colored pictures of fractals on the Internet.

PLATONIC SOLIDS

Platonic Solids were named after the philosopher Plato (427-347 BCE) even though Pythagoras, who used them much earlier, called them perfect solids. To be a Platonic Solid, each figure must have the same number of shapes that meet at each corner. All these shapes are naturally found in crystals.

Platonic Solids are considered part of Sacred Geometry because the Greeks felt they were an important part of nature and the energy fields around the body. To work with them connects us to a higher spiritual level.

PLATONIC SOLIDS – MAGICAL SHAPES

NAME	# OF SIDES	SYMBOL	COMPONENTS
TETRAHEDRON	4	FIRE	3 EQUILATERAL TRIANGLES AT EACH CORNER
CUBE	6	EARTH	3 SQUARES AT EACH CORNER
OCTAHEDRON	8	AIR	4 EQUILATERAL TRIANGLES AT EACH CORNER
DODECAHEDRON	12	WATER	3 REGULAR PENTAGONS AT EACH CORNER
ICOSAHEDRON	20	UNIVERSE	5 EQUILATERAL TRIANGLES AT EACH CORNER

ACADEMIC INTEGRATION
GEOMETRY IN ART - PAINTINGS OF VINCENT VAN GOGH

Vincent Van Gogh was born in Holland on March 30, 1853. His dad was a preacher and his mother came from a family of bookbinders. He had three younger sisters and two brothers. The artist loved flowers and animals, growing up among the cornfields and pine forests - themes reflected in many of his paintings. He began to draw in 1864 while attending boarding school. Before becoming an artist, he was a preacher, bookseller, teacher and art dealer. Those who mentored him as an artist were Gaughin, Seurat, Pissarro and Rousseau.

Van Gogh was not successful during his life. He survived on money from his family, particularly his brother Theo. Often he went hungry to buy paint instead of food. Some accounts of his life say he sold only one painting. Perhaps the cause was due to his mental illness, epilepsy and depression. Much of his life was spent in an asylum where he died in 1890 by his own hand.

His paintings fell into two periods. In the first half of his life, they were dark and sad. During the other half, he painted bright pictures.

His finest works were produced in less than three years, many of them reflecting his struggles with illness. He produced over 2,000 works during the last ten years of his life, the best in the final two years. Imagine what he could have produced if he lived longer!

Surf the Internet and find these paintings in color by Van Gogh: *Starry Night, Irises* and *Vase with Twelve Sunflowers.*

STARRY NIGHT

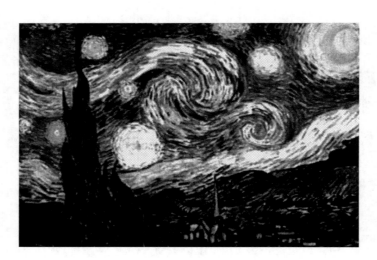

Starry Night is one of Van Gogh's best known paintings. The night sky is ablaze with spirals rolling over the sleepy town below. The bright windows in houses create a sense of warmth, comfort and seclusion. One can imagine the town's people snug inside their warm houses on a cold night while the stars and moon look over them. The steeple tries to reach heaven, but the tree or bushes seem to reach it better and appear larger when compared to other objects. The curving lines in the sky are wide and full, giving greater depth to the painting.

Note the thick globs of paint, sweeping brush strokes and color combinations. His placement of objects is clever. The bush on the left is large, balanced by sloping hills and fiery moon on the right. The sky illustrates how small humanity is but it is part of the larger universe. The painting, a product of his imagination, was done in 1889 while in an asylum before his death at age 37.

IRISES

Van Gogh also painted *Irises* while in an asylum. In the last year of his life, he actually produced 130 pictures. The irises in the painting grew on the hospital grounds. The artist studied their unique movement, creating a variety of curving waves and lines. They show divided areas with clear colors overflowing the garden's border.

His brother, Theo, wrote about the painting, "It stretches the eye from afar. It is a beautiful study full of air and life." The first owner of the painting, art critic Octave Mirceau, remarked, "How well he has understood the exquisite nature of flowers." Is it any wonder? Flowers were Van Gogh's favorite subject.

Ironically, he never received money for his paintings. In 1987, *Irises* sold at an auction for 48 million dollars, plus 10% to the auction house, totaling 53.9 million.

VASE WITH TWELVE SUNFLOWERS

Paintings of sunflowers by Van Gogh are considered among his most famous works. What few people realize is that he created a series of paintings on sunflowers. In addition to *Vase with Twelve Sunflowers*, there is also a painting titled *Vase with Fifteen Sunflowers*.

Some of the sunflower paintings bear the same title with minor differences barely noted on flower petals, centers of the flower or various colors schemes. What is remarkable is that each piece is a unique work of art.

The colors of the sunflowers shown here range from vibrant bright yellow to wilting brown. The life of the painting comes from inside each flower. One feels their movement from various stages of fresh flowers to wilted flowers to dry flowers. The spiral design is most evident in each sunflower center.

This painting, like many of his others sold at auction, went for millions of dollars. During his lifetime, Vincent remarked, "It is not my fault that my pictures don't sell, but one day people will know that they are worth more than the materials I used to paint them." That day certainly arrived.

SACRED GEOMETRY – CATHEDRAL ARCHITECTURE - CHARTRES

Sacred geometry is found in nature, art, music, science and especially architecture. Some of the greatest architecture is found in many cathedrals built in the middle ages. These creations are the results of deep mathematical thought, great discipline, creative planning and centuries of hard work. One surviving architectural masterpiece is Chartres Cathedral in France. It is ranked as one of the three best examples of Gothic French architecture. Chartres is discussed briefly here because it was designated as a pilgrimage church and contains one of the oldest surviving labyrinths.

The original architect of the Cathedral is unknown. How the builders measured the span of the nave or even if it would work in the first place remains a mystery. The basic floor plan is in the form of a cross.

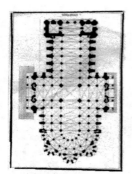

The cathedral was demolished by fire twice, once in 1134 and again in 1197. The church was rebuilt in less than 100 years (1220) which was an outstanding record compared to medieval standards.

The church became the center of various activities for the people of this quiet town. It was often a marketplace where they sold cloth, vegetables, wood, meat and wine. At times, the church was also used as a hospital and school.

In the process of building the design, a new architectural feature was adopted called

flying buttresses. Because of the two previous fires, a stone roof was built instead of a wooden one. The stone was heavy and pressed down on the walls which pushed them outward. Flying buttresses were built to brace the outer wall from pushing apart from the weight of the vault and steeples.

Note the pyramidal structure of the spires. One is 349' and the other is 377'. Arches also grace the structure both inside and outside.

Stained glass windows in most Gothic Cathedrals served many purposes. In general they contributed to the beauty of the building and allowed light into the interior of the structure. In the Middle Ages, light was associated with God. Less known is the fact that the designs told a story. Many people at that time in history could not read, so biblical stories were told from the images in the window as a means of education. There are 176 stained glass windows at Chartres. Two significant art structures in the cathedral are the Rose Window and the eleven-circuit labyrinth. The three rose windows are world famous. The center of the labyrinth contains a design that is referred to as rose petals. When the sun penetrates through the Rose Window at a certain time during the day, the design superimposes itself on the six rose petals at the center of the labyrinth. Whether this was the original intent of the builders is unknown.

MODERN ARCHITECTURE – GATEWAY TO THE WEST

Great architecture is not limited to any one particular era or culture. An amazing architectural feat in our own century is the stainless steel "Gateway Arch" in St. Louis, Missouri, a structure that stands 630' high, making it the tallest monument in the United States. Standing on the banks of the Mississippi River, it represents the Gateway to the West.

A national competition was held in 1947-1948 to design a monument to honor St. Louis' role in the westward expansion of the United States during the 19th century (1803-1890). The architect, Eero Saarinen, won the competition. Construction began in 1963 and ended two years later at a cost of 13 million dollars.

The two bases are equilateral triangles with 54' long sides that taper to the top with 17' on each side. It is considered the most structurally-sound arch shape. The arch weight 17,246 tons with 1900 tons of stainless steel.

To ensure that the arch would join at the top, the margin of error for failure was 1/64th of an inch. Visitors at the monument watch a movie of the crane lifting the final piece of structure, with thousands of people below holding their breath, waiting and hoping the last piece fits perfectly. When it did, there was great joy at this engineering marvel. The arch sways in the wind at a maximum of 18 inches, 9 inches each way, in a 150 mph wind. The normal sway is a half an inch. Millions of tourists visit the site and travel to the observation tower in small inner cable cars to view the scene from the top.

Eero Saarinen, the architect of the Gateway Arch, was born in Helsinki, Finland and immigrated to the United States in 1923. He studied architecture at Yale and graduated in 1934. Other great architectural projects by Eero Saarinen are the terminals in the John F. Kennedy Airport in NY, and Dulles International Airport in Washington, D.C.

So much more can be written about Sacred Geometry. Perhaps these few pages will build an interest in and appreciation of the many geometrical structures found in the human body, the Universe, art, music and architecture and lead the student to delve more fully into other great works of arts.

CLASS ART GALLERY PROJECT

Create a classroom Art Gallery Fair containing pictures of some of the following works of art, those mentioned throughout this book, or others of your own choice and creation. Be ready to explain an artistic point of view of your selection to visitors of the gallery.

1. Different labyrinth designs from around the world.

2. Pictures of weather patterns.

3. Computer designed fractals and fractals from nature.

4. Famous paintings from the Louvre Museum in Paris.

5. Two, three, or multi-dimensional geometric designs.

6. Pyramids.

7. Cathedrals.

8. Geometric designs from nature.

9. Ancient architecture: Stonehenge, Parthenon, Acropolis.

10. Modern architecture.

CHAPTER 6

HOW TO WALK A FINGER LABYRINTH

INTRODUCTION AND PERFORMANCE OBJECTIVES

An in-ground, portable labyrinth may not always be available to walk or some people may have a handicap which prevents them from walking a labyrinth with their feet. As an alternative, finger labyrinths are available in various sizes and shapes, including a left-and-right-handed one walked at the same time, thus enabling folks to circle the labyrinth conveniently with their fingers.

A finger labyrinth, or lap labyrinth as it is sometimes called, is made from many different materials: plastic, pewter, ceramic and various types of cloth and wood. The cost depends on the type of material used to make it. The finger labyrinth is walked in the same manner as a full-sized labyrinth, except the path is traced with a finger rather than walked with the feet. The path is compressed into the material enabling the user to slide the finger more effectively.

At the completion of this chapter, students will
- be aware of a variety of finger labyrinths and how to walk them.
- walk the left-and-right-handed finger labyrinths together.
- compare the differences between walking a labyrinth with the feet and with the finger.
- introduce the concept of chakras, their functions and connections.
- integrate language arts on how to write a paragraph.

ADVANTAGES OF FINGER LABYRINTHS

The advantages of using a finger labyrinth are many. They can be:
- Carried anywhere: pocket, briefcase, pocket book.
- Walked with eyes closed.
- More affordable.
- Held in the hand or placed on one's lap.
- Used as a teaching tool before walking a full-sized labyrinth.
- Available for those who are ill or cannot walk.
- Easily handled by children.
- Substituted in the absence of larger labyrinths.
- Made of lightweight materials.

HOW TO WALK A FINGER LABYRINTH

PREPARATION

Find a comfortable position.

Uncross legs and arms.

Center yourself by relaxing and taking deep breaths.

Let go of worries and concerns.

Be aware of how your body feels.

Remain open to whatever occurs.

FINGER TRACING TO THE CENTER

Use either right or left hand.

Place one or more fingers at the labyrinth opening.

Slowly trace the path to its center.

CENTER OF LABYRINTH

Pause, relax and take deep breaths.

Be aware of how you feel.

Ask yourself, what is the message received at this time?

Leave the center when ready.

RETURN

Return on the same path.

Think how to integrate the message received into your life.

Finger labyrinths come in a variety of sizes and shapes. Some finger labyrinths are walked with a stylus that fits into the labyrinth path.

FINGER LABYRINTH WALK

While listening to relaxing music, slowly walk the finger labyrinth that follows, using the instructions explained earlier in the chapter.

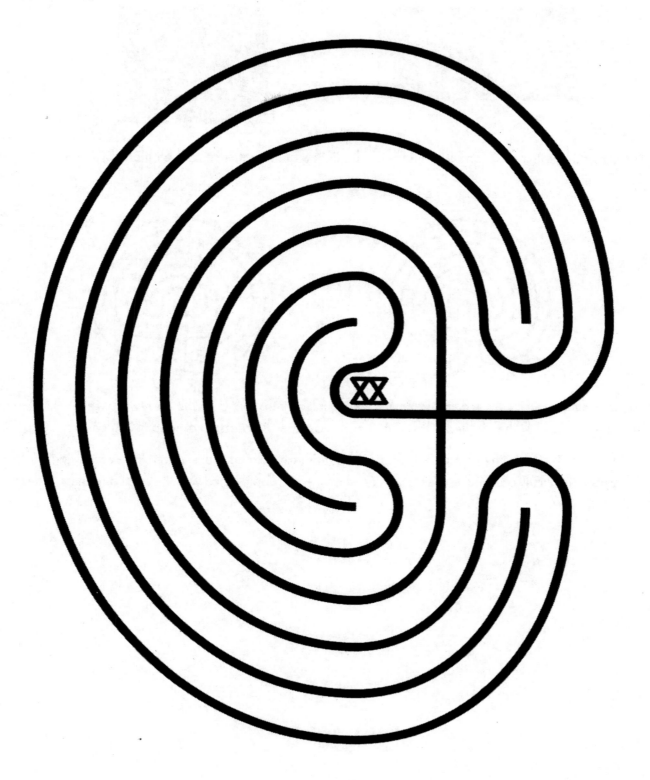

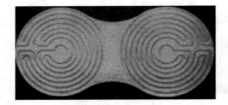

WALKING A LEFT-AND RIGHT-HANDED LABYRINTH TOGETHER

Some finger labyrinths are made to use with both the left hand and the right hand at the same time.

Note that the entrance to one labyrinth is on the right and the entrance to the other labyrinth is on the left.

Left entrance

Right entrance

Secure on a flat surface the left-and-right handed finger labyrinths found on the next two pages. While listening to relaxing music, walk the two labyrinths together. Follow the directions explained in this chapter.

Letting your fingers do the walking is a different labyrinth experience, but is as effective as walking with one's feet. The benefits are as powerful as their larger counterpart when approached with the same openness and respect.

LEFT-HANDED LABYRINTH

RIGHT-HANDED LABYRINTH

SEVEN-CIRCUIT CHAKRA-COLORED LABYRINTH

When using a seven-circuit finger labyrinth like the one on the previous page, it may be difficult to stay on the correct circuit because they are all white. It is so easy for the finger to slip into another circuit. Because of this, the finger labyrinth requires concentration and focus. Occasionally you will see a labyrinth where each circuit is a specific color. Certainly this would be much easier to finger walk.

THE ENERGY CENTERS OF THE BODY

Each circuit is a different color and corresponds to the seven energy centers that nourish certain parts of the body. These energy sources are called chakras. The same energy that flows through life also flows through the body.

The energy centers are responsible for our mental, physical, emotional and spiritual well being. They help balance the inner world with the outer world. Their purpose is to bring together all parts of life to create a well-balanced individual in body, mind and spirit.

The chakras are also connected to the days of the week, notes on a musical scale, colors and planets. The chart on the next page shows an outline of these connections in addition to the functions of the chakras.

CHAKRAS OF THE BODY AND THEIR CONNECTIONS

NUMBER, MUSICAL NOTE	BODY ORGAN	COLOR	DAY OF THE WEEK	PLANET	FUNCTION
7 - C	CROWN	VIOLET	MONDAY	SUN	AWARENESS, UNDERSTANDING
6 - D	EYE	INDIGO	WEDNESDAY	MOON	INTELLIGENCE, INTUITION
5 - E	THROAT	BLUE	FRIDAY	MERCURY	CREATIVITY, COMMUNICATION
4 - F	HEART	GREEN	SUNDAY	VENUS	LOVE, COMPASSION
3 - G	STOMACH	YELLOW	TUESDAY	MARS	STRENGTH, CONTROL, WILL
2 - A	NAVEL	ORANGE	THURSDAY	JUPITER	EMOTIONS, PROCREATION
1 - B	BASE OF SPINE	RED	SATURDAY	SATURN	LIMITATION, SURVIVAL GROUNDING

Color the labyrinth according to the chakra colors and walk the labyrinth with your finger. Was it easier? Why?

1 = Red, 2 = Orange, 3 = Yellow, 4 = Green, 5 = Blue, 6 = Indigo, 7 = Purple.

ACADEMIC INTEGRATION – LANGUAGE ARTS – WRITING A PARAGRAPH

Why do students cringe when asked to write a paragraph? Possibly two reasons answer this question. The first is that the writer believes the first attempt must be perfect. Even experienced writers edit, change and rewrite again and again. That is why they become good at it. As one learns to read by reading, one learns to write by writing. It is a gradual learning process that becomes better with practice. The second reason is that many students feel they need more preparation before writing a paragraph. Confidence grows with more understanding of the subject. A paragraph has about five to eight sentences with a very simple structure.

TOPIC SENTENCE	- introduces the subject or main idea. - captures the interest of the reader immediately.
SUPPORTING SENTENCES	- consists of details, facts, examples, ideas, descriptions, and comparisons that support the topic sentence.
CONCLUDING SENTENCE	- summarizes thoughts, gives a solution, states a conclusion or restates the topic sentence.

Begin by writing a simple paragraph. An outline on the subject of getting a GED diploma might look this.

Topic Sentence	The value of a GED.
Supporting Sentences	What subjects are tested? What are the writer's weakest and strongest subjects?
Concluding Sentence	The time to get a GED diploma is now.

On the first attempt at writing the paragraph, do not be concerned with correct spelling or grammar. They can be corrected later. The important thing is to get the words out of the head and onto the paper. Below is a sample paragraph on the subject of a GED diploma.

TOPIC SENTENCE – I know I can't do anything in life without a high school daploma.

SUPPORTING SENTENCES – I hope to get my GED at this school. The test has five parts, reading, language arts, social studies, sceince and math. four of the subjects is easy for me. English is hard. The second part of the language arts test is writing an esay on something familar. I take classes now where I can get help and should take advantage of it.

CONCLUDING SENTENCE – Guess I better pay attention on how to write a paragraph since an esay in made up of many paragraphs.

PROOFREADING AND PUTTING IT ALL TOGETHER

Now is the time to proofread and make corrections.

I know I can't do anything in life without a high school daploma. I hope to get my GED at this school. The test has five parts, reading, language arts, social studies, sceince and math. four of the subjects is easy for me. English is hard. The second part of the language arts test is writing an esay on something familar. I take classes now where I can get help and should take advantage of it. Guess I better pay attention on how to write a paragraph since an esay is made up of many paragraphs.

EXERCISES

Proofread and rewrite the paragraph correctly. Can you find the six errors?

_____

_____

_____

_____

_____

_____

_____

_____

_____

_____

_____

_____

Arrange the number of these sentences according to topic sentence, supporting sentences and concluding sentence.

A common rule is that the letter "i" goes before "e" except after "c". Sentences begin with a capital letter. Correct spelling, grammar and punctuation are important in writing a paragraph. A colon is used with a series of items that have one or more commas. Knowledge of spelling rules help. These are only a few punctuation rules out of many yet to learn. Although there are many rules for spelling, make friends with a dictionary.

_____

_____

_____

_____

_____

_____

_____

ANOTHER PARAGRAPH EXAMPLE

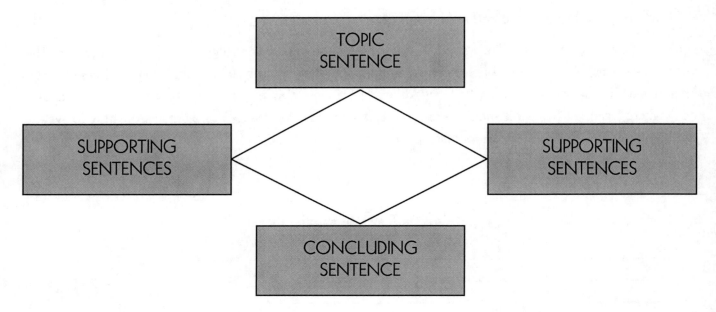

TOPIC SENTENCE

Birthdays celebrated on a labyrinth are really exciting, different and lots of fun for everyone.

SUPPORTING SENTENCES

A birthday labyrinth walk is easy to plan. Celebrate with enough balloons for each person participating. Before the walk, place the balloons in the center of the labyrinth. Each person who walks takes a balloon from the center for the outward journey. When all have completed the walk, each person presents a balloon and gives a special birthday wish to the one celebrating.

CLOSING SENTENCE

I think I would like to celebrate my birthday with a special birthday labyrinth walk.

EXERCISE

Write a paragraph on one of the following topics.

Advantages of having a finger labyrinth.

Experience of walking a right-and-left finger labyrinth together.

Difference between a finger, portable or in-ground labyrinth.

Chakras and their purposes.

Any other topic that is familiar to you.

WRITE A SHORT PARAGRAPH OUTLINE

_____
_____
_____
_____
_____
_____
_____
_____
_____
_____
_____
_____
_____
_____
_____
_____
_____

Write a paragraph first on scrap paper. After editing, write a final copy below.

_____
_____
_____
_____
_____
_____
_____
_____
_____
_____
_____
_____
_____
_____
_____
_____
_____

CHAPTER 7

THE TECHNIQUE OF DOWSING AND CONSTRUCTING A SEVEN-CIRCUIT LABYRINTH

PERFORMANCE OBJECTIVES AND ACADEMIC OUTLINE

The location of a labyrinth is important for any labyrinth experience to be worthwhile. The site should draw people to walk it and to feel the earth's energy. The environment should be pleasant, quiet and attractive, within an atmosphere that fosters relaxation, focusing and meditation. This chapter discusses two techniques of dowsing on how to find an appropriate labyrinth location and instructions on how to construct a simple seven-circuit labyrinth. However, like any type of construction, adequate preparation is essential, particularly in the area of mathematical measurements. Many questions must be considered prior to building a labyrinth. What is important in this endeavor is to keep the process simple; find a good location, discuss labyrinth questions, draw the model on paper, then proceed to build the labyrinth.

Upon completion of this chapter, students will:

- learn the techniques of dowsing to find a favorable labyrinth site.

- learn facts about water, the water cycle and read water poetry.

- consider relevant labyrinth questions and draw a labyrinth blueprint.

- review linear measurements and their conversions.

- follow directions by drawing a labyrinth from the seed pattern.

DOWSING TECHNIQUES

Dowsing is the practice of searching for water, metal or other objects underground using an instrument called a dowsing rod. Other names for dowsing are divining and doodlebugging. Dowsing has been around for thousands of years and is still practiced today. Those who practice this technique are call dowsers.

Two methods of dowsing are used today. In the first method, dowsers use an instrument such as a rod, stick or pendulum to find what is called primary water. Primary water is found deep within the Earth. A deep well is an example of where primary water is located. Should primary water exist underground, the rod or Y-shaped stick moves where water is present. This method is effective about 95% of the time.

DOWSING ROD

PENDULUM

Water above the Earth's surface is called ground water. It differs from primary water because it rests above the Earth's surface in rivers, lakes and oceans. Ground water is part of the water cycle that includes evaporation, cloud formation and rain.

Ground Water Flow

The second manner of dowsing relates to the Earth's energies. Dowsers believe the Earth possesses electromagnetic energy that affects the human body. Electromagnetic energy happens when you move on a metal surface and then touch someone, you get an electric shock. Many believe our senses are more powerful than we think and the body can also detect the Earth's energies.

Some people believe dowsing doesn't work because it can't be proven scientifically. Science wants reasons, explanations and proof. Dowsing is not a science. It is a technique.

The purpose of dowsing is to unite human energy with the energy of the Earth. Labyrinths are constructed above underground water so the energies of both Earth and body can more easily guide us in the right direction. Before building a labyrinth, use a Y-shaped stick (or coat hanger) to locate underground water in order to determine the best location for a labyrinth.

QUESTIONS TO CONSIDER BEFORE CONSTRUCTING A LABYRINTH

1. What is the motive for building a labyrinth?

2. For whom is the labyrinth intended?

3. What criteria are used to determine the location of the labyrinth?

4. How is the location of the labyrinth determined?

5. What is the labyrinth design: 3, 5, 7 or 11 circuits?

6. Is the labyrinth permanent or portable?

7. Is the entrance to the labyrinth on the right or left side?

8. How many people will the labyrinth accommodate at one time?

9. What materials will be used: brick, gravel, lime, tile, stone, mounds, cement, pavement, granite, terrazzo, painted stones, wood blocks, mowed grass, flags or masking tape?

10. What is the overall size of the labyrinth?

11. What is the desired measurement for the walking path?

12. What is the desired width for the center of the labyrinth?

13. What is the width of the line that separates the path into circuits?

14. What space is available outside the labyrinth for benches, bushes, flowers or trees?

15. How many people (staff, volunteers) will work on the construction?

16. What type of on-going maintenance is required?

DRAW THE MODEL ON PAPER FIRST
AND
DEVELOP A CONSTRUCTION TIMELINE.

MAKING A SEVEN-CIRCUIT LABYRINTH
PRELIMINARY MEASUREMENTS

Measurements for a labyrinth depend on the size of available space. The illustration of a 40' labyrinth construction below is only a sample. The same process can be used for any size.

1. Place the measuring point (X) in the lower section of the space since most of the labyrinth lines are above it.

2. Determine the width of the walking path (20").

3. Determine the width of the border line (8").

4. Determine the size of the center of the labyrinth (6').
   (3' on each side of the X measuring point).

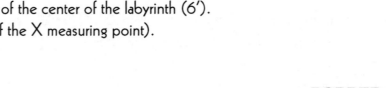
BORDER 8"

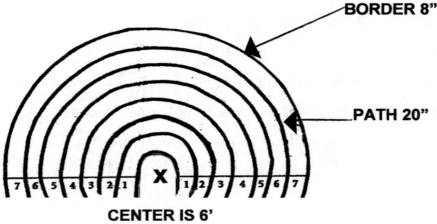
PATH 20"

7 6 5 4 3 2 1 **X** 1 2 3 4 5 6 7

CENTER IS 6'

TOTAL MEASUREMENTS

Center is 6'	=	72"
16 borders at 8"	=	128"
14 turns at 20"	=	280"
TOTAL INCHES		480"

TOTAL FEET = 40' **LABYRINTH**

5. Obtain a dowel, plunger or other appropriate tool. The wood is placed in the ground and the plunger on a surface.

6. Purchase a 25' nylon rope or chain. Loop material loosely over the tool to allow it to move easily.

7. Make the first mark 3' from the edge of the tool to provide space for the center.

   Make another mark at 28" from the end of the 3' mark (20" for the path width and 8" for the width for the line border).

   28" 3'

8. Make a total of seven 28" marks from the 3' mark. There are eight lines in all, one at 3' and 7 at 28".

9. Place the plunger or dowel on the X. Lay the rope straight down and rotate the rope clockwise to form the top half of the labyrinth. As you go along, mark the labyrinth lines to correspond with each of the eight marks on the rope. Markings may be done in tape, lime or paint.

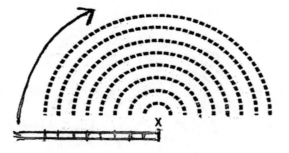

Another option would be to do one path at a time with a shorter rope of 3' followed by one mark of 28". The advantage of the longer rope with 3' and seven markings of 28" is that eight people can tape at one time as the rope turns.

10. Fill spaces between tape to make a solid line. The top half of the labyrinth should now be complete. Mark the letters B and C as shown in the diagram.

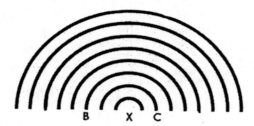

11. Connect the lines on each side of B with a half circle. Be sure to keep a space of 28". Place the plunger on point B. Move the rope to the left to connect with the semi-circles on top. Place pieces of tape to correspond with the marks on the rope.

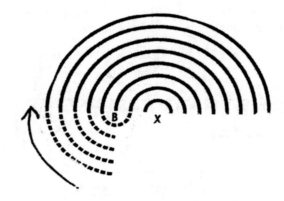

12. Connect the lines on each side of C with a half circle. Maintain the same width size of 28" Place the plunger on point C. Move the rope to the right to connect with the semi-circle on top. Place pieces of tape to correspond with the marks on the rope.

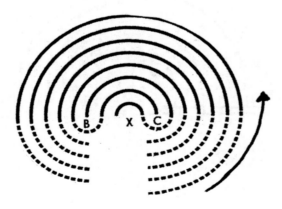

13. Fill spaces between pieces of tape to form solid lines in the left and right section on the bottom half of the labyrinth.

14. Extend the horizontal center line downward as shown in the diagram.

15. Connect the lower left and right lines nearest the center to form a vertical line as shown in the design.

16. Connect the lines above and below the letter A. Maintain the same path width of 28".

17. Connect the lines above and below the letter D with a half circle. Maintain the 28" space.

18. Connect the outer line on the right to meet the horizontal line extending from the center. Maintain the same path width of 28".

The lines of tape, paint or lyme can be used as a guide for a permanent border of rocks, shrubs, bricks, small flags, etc.

THE LABYRINTH IS NOW COMPLETE.

ACADEMIC INTEGRATION - THE WATER CYCLE

How does ground water function in the many processes that make up the water cycle, also known as the hydrologic cycle? The water cycle consists of six components: evaporation, condensation, precipitation, surface runoff, infiltration and transpiration.

1. EVAPORATION – Liquid water in oceans, ponds, lakes, swamps, rivers and plants is heated by the sun and evaporates. Temperature causes the liquid state to change to a vapor or gaseous state.

2. CONDENSATION – The vapor from evaporation rises and condenses into millions of tiny droplets that form clouds in the sky or fog on the ground.

3. PRECIPITATION – Depending on the temperature or atmospheric pressure, droplets fall from the clouds in the form of rain, sleet, snow or hail called precipitation.

AS A RESULT OF EVAPORATION, CONDENSATION AND PRECIPITATION,
THE WATER RETURNS TO THE EARTH.

4. SURFACE RUNOFF – The water that returns to the Earth as precipitation runs off the surface of the land into streams, ponds, etc., and eventually into the ocean.

5. INFILTRATION – Water not absorbed into rivers, etc., infiltrates into the soil and rock layers and becomes ground water.

6. TRANSPIRATION – When plants absorb the water from the soil, the water goes into the roots, up the stem into the leaves, adding to the water vapor in the air. The evaporation through the leaves is transpiration... Then the water cycle begins all over again.

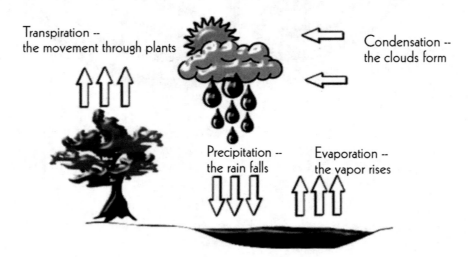

Transpiration --
the movement through plants

Condensation --
the clouds form

Precipitation --
the rain falls

Evaporation --
the vapor rises

As the water cycle demonstrates, water is part of an inter-connected process. New water isn't fed into the Earth during the water cycle. The amount of water on the Earth is the same amount as there was when the Earth came into existence. The water available today contains the same molecules that dinosaurs drank. What we put in the ground becomes part of our water, what we send into the sky becomes part of our drinking water. No wonder ecologists are continually asking for cleaner air and water.

Over 70% of the planet Earth is water. The U.S. Environmental Protection Agency (EPA) states that, "Nearly 97% of the world's water is salty or otherwise undrinkable. Another 2% is locked in ice caps and glaciers. That leaves 1% for all of humanity's needs — all its agriculture, residential, manufacturing, community and personal needs. A person can live about a month without food, but only about a week without water. The average total home water use for each person in the U.S. is about 50 gallons a day."

Around 70% of the human body is water. Water regulates body temperature, carries nutrients and oxygen to cells, cushions joints, protects organs and tissues and removes wastes. Water is our lifeline.

POETRY - WHERE WILL I FIND WATER TODAY?

In the beauty of the sea, with its ebb and flow,

In the soothing presence of a gentle rain.

In deep, hidden springs that encourage me to life.

In a sacred space, risking the search for living water.

In conserving that others may simply live.

Where will I find water today?

Where will all other creatures find water today

and down through seven generations?

Is there a relationship between my use of water

and the survival of the rest of creation?

Where will I find water today?

Approximately 1.5 billion people have no access to clean water

and 2.6 billion lack access to basic sanitation.

Thomas Barry tells us, "Earth cannot recover from the present human

assault without the assistance of humans themselves.

The human community and the natural world will go into the future as a

single, sacred community or we will both perish in the desert."

Where will I find water today?

How much do I need?

Ann Lynch

TO WATER

As tears, you cradle sadness and pain,

Then drop into Earth, only to rise again.

Recycled, you join communities of drops

And become oceans, rivers, and puddles.

You are home to whales and betta fish.

No creature is too great or too small

To contain or be held by you.

From the beginning,

You are life blood of Earth and all that lives.

Liquid star stuff,

You surge through my veins

And wrap around my spirit,

Surging sea-like into a song of praise.

I thank you.

I thank the Creator for you,

And pray that I will always attend to you

With great love.

Sally Marsh

MATH – CONVERTING LINEAR MEASUREMENT REVIEW

◀ 1 foot (ft.) = 12 inches (in.)

3 feet = 1 yard (yd.)

1 yard = 36 inches

5,280 feet = 1 mile (mi.)

CONVERSION RULES

1. Conversion means to change. To convert measurement, either multiply or divide.

2. Multiply to change from a greater measurement to a lesser measurement.

3. Divide to change from a lesser measurement to a greater measurement.

EXAMPLES

1. CHANGE 4 FEET TO INCHES.

a. Multiply because a foot is greater than an inch.

b. Find the number of inches in 1 foot: 1 foot = 12 inches.

c. Multiply 4 feet times 12 inches = 48 inches.

2. CHANGE 144 INCHES TO YARDS

a. Divide because an inch is less than a yard.

b. Find the number of inches in 1 yard: 1 yard = 36 inches.

c. Divide 144 inches by 36 = 4 yards.

LINEAR MEASUREMENT EXERCISES

Write whether you multiply or divide in each of the following:

feet to inches _____   feet to yards _____

yards to feet _____   feet to miles   _____

inches to feet _____   yards to inches _____

inches to yards _____   miles to feet _____

CONVERT THESE MEASUREMENTS

1 yard = _____ inches

72 inches = _____ yards

36 inches = _____ feet

3 feet = _____ yards

12 feet = _____ inches

8 yards = _____ feet

1 mile = _____ feet

8 yards = _____ inches

3 miles = _____ feet

10,560 feet = _____ miles

Convert these labyrinth measurements from inches to feet.

4' center of labyrinth	=	_____	INCHES
16 border lines at 4"	=	_____	INCHES
14 walking turns at 16"	=	_____	INCHES

TOTAL INCHES _____

NUMBER OF FEET _____

FOLLOWING DIRECTIONS SKILLS

Following directions is an important function in daily living: reading recipes or blueprints, sewing clothes from patterns, assembling gadgets and toys, setting alarms, driving cars (GPS), using medicine, playing games, planting flowers, making cement and much, much more.

Reading directions is one thing, following them is another. Too often, directions are carelessly read or not enough attention is given to following them correctly.

Listening is a very important part of following directions. If directions are in sequence, missing a single step throws off the successful completion of the whole. Although everyone knows the importance of following directions, mastering the skill takes practice. The following exercises are offered to help strengthen one's ability to follow directions.

EXERCISES

1. Make a square in the middle of the paper.

2. Place a dot in the middle of the square.

3. On the right, lower corner of the square, draw an arrow downward.

4. At the point of the arrow, draw a circle.

5. In the middle of the circle, write the first letter of your last name.

6. From the dot in the middle of the square, draw a line to each of the four corners.

7. On the upper left-hand corner of the square, draw an arrow upward.

8. At the tip of the arrow, draw a triangle.

9. In the middle of the triangle, write the first letter of your first name.

Have students create their own designs and read them to others. Giving directions helps build attention-to-detail and correct sequence skills.

Complete on lined paper.

1. Write your first name on the last line of the paper at the left-hand margin.

2. On the first line of the paper, write the numbers 1 through 9. Start at the left and print the numbers. Leave a space between each number.

3. Circle the number 6.

4. Draw a star in the upper left-hand corner of the page.

5. Fold your paper in half the long way.

6. Open up the paper, than fold it the opposite way.

7. Use the tip of your pencil to poke a hole in the center of the paper (the place where the two folds meet).

8. Draw a heart around the hole you made in the paper.

9. Write the first initial of your last name in the upper right-hand corner of the page.

10. On the last line of the page, write the word done near the right margin.

LABYRINTH FOLLOWING DIRECTIONS SKILLS

The instructor will review vocabulary words first: horizontal, vertical, arch and right angles; then read directions to students.

1. Draw a cross.

2. Add right angles on the left and right, top and bottom of the cross, with the open part of the angle facing outward.

3. Add four dots on the left and right, top and bottom angles to form the basic seed pattern.

4. Connect the top line of the cross with the top line of the right angle, making an arch.

5. Make an arch by connecting the vertical top of the left angle with the top right dot.

6. Make an arch by connecting the top left dot with the horizontal line at the top of the right angle.

7. Make an arch by connecting the horizontal line on the top left angle with the right horizontal line on the cross.

8. Make an arch by connecting the left horizontal line of the cross with the horizontal line on the lower right angle.

9. Make an arch by connecting the horizontal line of the bottom left angle with the lower left dot.

10. Connect the bottom left dot to the vertical line of the bottom right angle, making an arch.

11. Connect the vertical line of the bottom left angle to the vertical line of the cross.

LABYRINTH PROJECTS

1. Write a labyrinth story about your labyrinth experiences.

2. Write essays on the process of building a labyrinth from beginning to end.

3. Write a school newsletter. Interview other students about their reactions to building a labyrinth.

4. Have a panel discussion about the labyrinth; its history, how to walk it, etc.

5. Prepare a labyrinth walk for other students.

6. Plan a labyrinth walk with parents and children.

CHAPTER 8

LABYRINTH WALK CELEBRATIONS

INTRODUCTION AND PERFORMANCE OBJECTIVES

In previous chapters, many phases of the labyrinth were introduced while integrating them with relevant academic subjects. The focus of this chapter is to concentrate on planning actual labyrinth walks.

People walk the labyrinth for a variety of reasons. At times, certain themes can be suggested. Four themes introduced in this chapter are Self-esteem, Positive Thinking, Relaxation and Peace. The purpose of doing so is to provide a simple format that can be applied to any theme. The format includes background information on the theme, readings or poems to further develop the theme, the labyrinth walk, and a follow-up process after the walk on how to conclude the experience.

A fine line exists between presenting guidelines and allowing the labyrinth walk to flow freely and this must be recognized and honored first. More than enough material is included with each theme. An underlying principle in planning the endeavor is to keep the process simple.

At the conclusion of the chapter, students will:

- understand some steps in planning a labyrinth experience.

- be given ideas on enhancing an understanding of the theme.

- provide instructions on incorporating the theme into the walk.

- provide suggestions for a follow-up and concluding process.

SELF-ESTEEM LABYRINTH WALK CELEBRATION
BACKGROUND INFORMATION - THE MEANING OF SELF-ESTEEM

Self-esteem is the way you value and think about yourself as a human being. It is a feeling inside you that says YOU ARE IMPORTANT. Do you believe that you are a special and unique individual and worthy of happiness? Can you treat yourself as someone special?

> MOST FOLKS ARE ABOUT AS HAPPY AS THEY
> MAKE UP THEIR MINDS TO BE.
> ABRAHAM LINCOLN

Self-esteem also tells you what you think about other people. If you do not like yourself, how can you like others? You cannot give what you don't have. What kind of inner conversations do you have about yourself? Do you have doubts about your abilities? Do you compare yourself with others?

Self-esteem is built upon the experiences of success. When people succeed, they grow in self-confidence and are capable of facing the daily challenges of life. Beware of falling into the trap of mixing up who you are with what you do; value yourself as unique individuals who can make a contribution to the world.

SIGNS OF HEALTHY SELF-ESTEEM

Well-balanced people are recognized by many of the following healthy signs of self-esteem. The opposite behavior shows persons with low self-esteem.

- Forgive your mistakes and learn from them.

- Stop putting yourself or others down.

- Set reasonable goals.

- Move on in spite of setbacks or road blocks.

- Receive honest criticism graciously.

- Learn to laugh at yourself.

- Communicate openly and express your needs.

- Are unlikely to be defensive when questioned.

- Feel worthy of love and can love others.

- Look at situations in a positive manner.

- Are responsible and accountable for one's actions.

- Have hopes for the future.

- Balance work and fun.

- Are comfortable in the presence of others.

- Cope with the challenges of life.

DEVELOPMENT OF THE THEME - WAYS TO BUILD SELF-ESTEEM

Part of being human means that we are not perfect and that at times we will all make mistakes and do things of which we are not proud. Building healthy self-esteem means letting go of past mistakes and becoming a better person now. Thinking well of yourself requires practice. Here are some ways to build self-esteem.

- Become better at <u>ONE</u> little thing each day.

- Develop your talents and skills.

- Treat others as you wish to be treated.

- Have friends that make you feel good about yourself.

- Do something special for someone each day.

- Put yourself in situations where your self-esteem can grow.

- Try not to take yourself too seriously.

- Learn how to be your own best friend.

- Do things that you enjoy.

- Praise yourself when you do something good; praise others as well.

- Have good hobbies.

- Reward your successes.

- Know it is OK to be imperfect.

- Get plenty of sleep and eat healthy foods.

- Read good books, look for new ideas.

- Involve yourself in worthwhile activities.

- Free yourself of "shoulds". Do what is right for you and not what others think you "should" do.

- Learn new experiences that build self-esteem.

POEM - WHAT IS SUCCESS?

Ralph Waldo Emerson (1803-1882)

To laugh often and much;

To win the respect of intelligent people and the affection of children;

To earn the appreciation of honest critics

And endure the betrayal of false friends;

To appreciate beauty,

To find the best in others,

To leave the world a bit better; whether by a healthy child,

A garden patch, or a redeemed social condition;

To know that one life has breathed easier because you have lived.

This is to have succeeded.

THE LABYRINTH WALK ON SELF-ESTEEM

1. Review directions on how to walk the labyrinth (see Chapter 3).

a. While walking from the entrance of the labyrinth to the center, think of three or four ways to build self-esteem that you need to acquire. (Consult the list written earlier or add some of your own.)

b. At the center, select two of these traits to work on each day.

c. On the way out, decide how you can apply the traits in your daily life. For example, if you tend to put yourself or others down, stop and give compliments instead.

FOLLOW-UP PROCESS - WRITING EXERCISE AND DISCUSSION

1. The two self-esteem traits I chose to practice are:

_____

_____

_____

_____

_____

_____

_____

2. The ways in which I will practice these traits in my daily life are:

_____

_____

_____

_____

_____

_____

_____

_____

Share your answers on how you will build self-esteem with the group and how you will practice them in your daily life.

Ask for and gently receive helpful suggestions from others.

3. Conclude the labyrinth walk celebration with everyone reading together,
   I Celebrate Me.

I CELEBRATE ME

I am worth celebrating. I am worth everything.

I am unique, in the whole world there is only one me.

There is only one person with my

talents, experiences and gifts.

NO ONE MAY TAKE MY PLACE.

God created only one me, precious in God's sight.

I have immense potential to love, care, create, grow,

sacrifice —

IF I BELIEVE IN MYSELF.

It doesn't matter my age, or color, or

whether my parents loved me or not.

(Maybe they wanted to but were unable.)

It doesn't matter what I have been,

the things I've done, mistakes I've made, people I've hurt.

I AM FORGIVEN.

I am accepted, I am okay, I am loved in spite of everything.

So I love myself and nourish seeds within me.

I celebrate me. I begin now, start anew.

I give myself a new birth today.

I AM ME, AND THAT'S ALL I NEED TO BE.

This is a new beginning,

A new life given freely.

So I celebrate the miracles and

I CELEBRATE ME.

- (Author Unknown)

POSITIVE THINKING LABYRINTH WALK CELEBRATION
BACKGROUND INFORMATION - THE MEANING OF POSITIVE THINKING

The way we think is molded into our minds at a very early age. If you came from a happy home where you were supported, praised and loved, positive thinking is easier to identify and practice. If brought up in a negative atmosphere, where success was undermined or where difficult situations prevailed, positive thinking is much harder.

Our environment also greatly affects our way of thinking. Television and other news media bombard us with stories of daily wars, crimes, disasters and negative commentaries. The language of the streets, rap music and negative advertising seeps into our subconscious and overpowers our brain into thinking this is the norm. To receive negative energy is to let the power of negativity fester the mind, which in turn creates more failures and negative behavior. The way one thinks determines whether the behavior is negative or positive. Both require the same amount of energy, but the results are different. Thinking is a neutral power that can be directed in the right way. Thinking negatively can be changed. The first step is to identify the negativity. The second step is to do the inner work required to change it. It takes time and energy. Promise yourself NOW that you are going to avoid negative thinking. How? Consider these points.

- When you notice a negative thought, change it to a positive one; instead of saying I can't, say I can.

- Praise yourself and others.

- Keep the mind focused on important things.

- Be honest with yourself and others.

- Develop positive goals and actions.

- Appreciate as much as you can.

- Stop comparing yourself to others.

- Realize it is possible to choose how to act the right way.

- Educate yourself. Feed your mind with useful information.

- Live in the here and now.

- Focus more on what you want instead of what you don't want.

- Focus on what you have rather than what you want.

- Redefine failure. The only failure in life is NOT to learn from your experiences.

- Success is possible in every instance.

All our feelings, beliefs, and knowledge are based on our inner thoughts. How we act depends on the inner dialogues we have with ourself. We choose whether to have a negative or positive attitude. You are in control. Promise yourself to change your life. It can be done.

DEVELOPMENT OF THE THEME - THE POWER OF POSITIVE WORDS

Scientists tell us that four elements are necessary for survival: oxygen, water, food, and sleep. What these elements have in common is that they bring energy to the body. Scientists say that to have energy there must be vibrations. Everything that exists is in a state of vibration, which in turn becomes the source of our energy. Therefore, there is no existence or energy without vibration.

To understand a vibration, think of striking an object. You can almost hear the vibrations. The sounds of music or words are vibrations that enter the ears and are translated into messages.

Something is needed to transmit the energy of vibration throughout the body. Water is this element. Over 70% of the body is made up of water. Without water, the energy of vibrations is not able to flow through the body and keep it alive.

Dr. Masaru Emoto, a renowned Japanese scientist, wanted to prove how the power of water and words effect the body. He maintained that words used in everyday language greatly influence our lives. When the water in our body is exposed to the vibration of positive words, we experience well being and happiness. Likewise, when the body is exposed to the vibration of bad words, we experience a negative effect.

The manner in which Dr. Emoto proved his belief and position was through photography. He took a small amount of water and breathed positive words over it like thank you, I love you, you can do it, peace, etc. He froze the water drops into crystals and took photos. He then froze water exposed to negative words and made photographs. When comparing the photos, he noted quite a difference. The crystals exposed to positive words were more beautiful than the crystals exposed to negative words. This is understandable when one recognizes the calm that comes with a hot shower and a cool refreshing drink. He suggests reverencing water by saying thank you for the gift it brings to our body and the positive energy that comes with using positive words.

POSITIVE ENERGY OF LAUGHTER

Negative thoughts and words lead to stress and illness. So too, the lack of laughter leads to the same results. A good laugh dissolves tension, stress, anxiety, anger, grief, depression and pent-up emotions.

The most wasted day is the day in which we have not laughed. The average kindergarten child laughs about 300 times a day, while adults only laugh about 17 times. Do adults take life too seriously? To laugh at our mistakes dissolves them, or at least makes them bearable. William James, (1842-1910) said, "We don't laugh because we're happy, we are happy because we laugh." Laughter is a gift to help us cope with and smile through the difficulties of life.

For healthy living, we need a sense of humor. A sense of humor isn't only about telling jokes; it is the way in which we look at ourselves and the world. A wholesome sense of humor is not laughing at other people or making fun of them at their expense; it is about sharing the funny things that happen to us in the process of living. We can't control what happens to us, but we can change how we react to what happens to us and what we need to do about it. Laughter helps us roll with the punches that life brings our way. Laughter is therapy.

CHANGING THE NEGATIVE TO POSITIVE

Changing negative thoughts to positive ones is an art that requires practice.

Practice by changing these negative thoughts to positive ones.

1. I wish I were someone else.

_____

2. Nothing turns out right for me.

_____

3. I'll never use alcohol or drugs.

_____

4. I really wasn't a good student.

_____

5. Other people are better than I am.

_____

6. I can't give up my addiction.

_____

7. My family doesn't trust me.

_____

8. I wasn't thinking straight.

_____

9. That is too big a problem for me.

_____

10. I can't stand him, he brags too much.

_____

THE LABYRINTH WALK ON POSITIVE THINKING

As you enter the labyrinth and walk toward the center, think of some of the negative thoughts you have about yourself or another person.

When you get to the center, choose two negative thoughts you want to change. When you have one, leave the center of the labyrinth.

As you walk out the labyrinth, plan how to change the negative thought into a positive one.

FOLLOW-UP PROCEDURES - WRITING EXERCISE AND DISCUSSION

The two negative thoughts I chose to correct are:

_____

_____

I change these negative thoughts to positive ones:

_____

_____

The ways in which I will practice these positive thoughts daily are:

_____

_____

_____

Share your positive thought answers with the group and how you will practice them in your daily life. Ask for and gently receive helpful suggestions from others.

Close the labyrinth walk by reading together thoughts on positive thinking and laughter.

THOUGHTS ON POSITIVE THINKING AND LAUGHTER

◆ Laughter attracts joy, releases negativity and leads to healthy living.

• You cannot help yourself or others by focusing on the negative. You only add to the problem.

◆ The more you share your sense of humor, the more friends you will have.

• We all have the power to do greater things than we realize, and one of these powers is to know it can happen.

◆ Consciously resolve to laugh more frequently during the day.

• You were born to add value to the world and to be better today than you were yesterday.

◆ If you can laugh about something, you can live with it.

• Join the fun and foolishness of life so that laughter may ring throughout the universe.

◆ Laughter is the best medicine. Develop your sense of humor and you will find yourself more productive in life. He or she who laughs… lasts.

> ALL THAT WE ARE IS A RESULT OF WHAT WE HAVE THOUGHT.
> (BUDDHA 568-483 CE)

RELAXATION LABYRINTH WALK CELEBRATION
BACKGROUND INFORMATION - THE MEANING OF RELAXATION

Most people understand the meaning of relaxation first and foremost by experiencing its opposite: overwork, dis-ease or worry. Relaxation is the activity of providing relief or diversion from such feelings.

The world in which we live is chaotic and stressful. Our focus and priorities often become unbalanced and unclear, creating a sense of unrest. The pace of life is becoming faster and more stressful. Many people live cut off from the natural world and become dependent on machines and complex technologies. To continue a stressful way of life without regular relaxation or physical exercise leads to burnout and ill health.

Folks recognize the need to relax. Following through is often the problem. Excuses prevail: I'm too busy, there isn't enough time, or I'm tired. People must develop a mindset that says this is the most important priority of the day and make the time to do it.

Taking the time to relax reduces tensions, keeps stress under control and provides a healthy outlook on life. Methods and ways to relax are numerous: yoga, physical exercise, meditation, writing, reading, movies, sleeping, swimming, hobbies, massages, sports events, concerts, dancing, playing an instrument, listening to music, taking a hot shower or bath, walking, playing cards, focusing, centering, sailing, fishing, singing, poetry, crafts and much, much more.

Although these suggestions are worthwhile, for the busy, over-stressed person, it is just something else to do. In this case, an additional activity only adds to the stress. Many of the suggestions given above also cost money, which may not be affordable or practical to some. Each person has to select what is doable and affordable within his or her lifestyle.

However, there are many powerful ways to relax that cost nothing and take little time to do. One important way is to concentrate on your breathing. Try these two breathing exercises.

EXERCISE 1 - DEEP BREATHING

A. Close your eyes and take a deep breath, counting slowly, 1-2-3-4-5.

B. When the lungs feel full, let your breath roll out slowly, counting 5-4-3-2-1.

C. Do these steps several times, feeling the relaxation in your body.

D. If you start to think of something else, or become distracted, refocus your breathing. It will help you forget everything else.

EXERCISE 2 - SIGHING

A. Stand or sit straight and let your body relax.

B. Take a deep sigh from your diaphragm, filling your lungs. Do not lift the shoulders.

C. Slowly let out a deep sigh as the air leaves your lungs.

D. Repeat this six or seven times or until you have a deep feeling of relaxation.

DEVELOPMENT OF THE THEME - TAKE A DEEP BREATH by Chris Thomas

Breathing is something you probably don't think about. Yet if you bring awareness and attention to your breathing, you'll find it can help you in many ways. It can help you connect mind, body and spirit, release stress and tension, achieve a state of relaxation and gain some control over your emotional state.

In addition, by taking the time to observe your breathing, you can learn about how you deal with certain stressors in your life. Sometimes your breathing is calm, sometimes it is rapid, and sometimes you literally stop breathing and hold your breath. As you begin to become aware of your breathing, you'll start to recognize how important your breathing can be to your balance of body and mind.

Here is an exercise to help you become more aware of your breathing patterns. Find a comfortable location that is quiet and peaceful. Sit upright, close your eyes, and for a few minutes, slowly lift your shoulders up and down toward your ears.

Remember to relax your shoulders and continue the motion until your arms feel like they are just hanging. Keep your lips closed and tuck your chin slightly in your neck. Notice how your arms feel as they hang from your body. Are they heavier? Are they lighter? Keep taking deep and steady breaths, but don't strain your neck. Your goal is to become more aware of yourself and of your breathing in a natural state.

The next time you feel tense or in need of restored spirit, practice this technique. This simple breathing exercise takes no more than 10 minutes, a small expenditure of your precious time. But the benefits to your health and well-being may be longer lasting.

THE LABYRINTH WALK ON RELAXATION

Undoubtedly, one of the many powerful benefits of walking a labyrinth is relaxation and stress reduction. Walking the labyrinth helps maintain a healthy balance between work and play.

Breathing deeply before entering the labyrinth helps relieve stress. When you feel somewhat relaxed, begin to walk the labyrinth, breathing slowly. As you move toward the center, think of some of the tensions in your life. At the center, select one tension you want to relieve. While walking out of the labyrinth, think of how you can relax to lessen this tension.

FOLLOW-UP PROCEDURES - WRITING EXERCISE AND DISCUSSION

Study the sample relaxation chart on the next page. On the blank labyrinth below, write your own ways to relax in your daily environment. Share ideas. Conclude the walk by reciting together the poem, *Nature*.

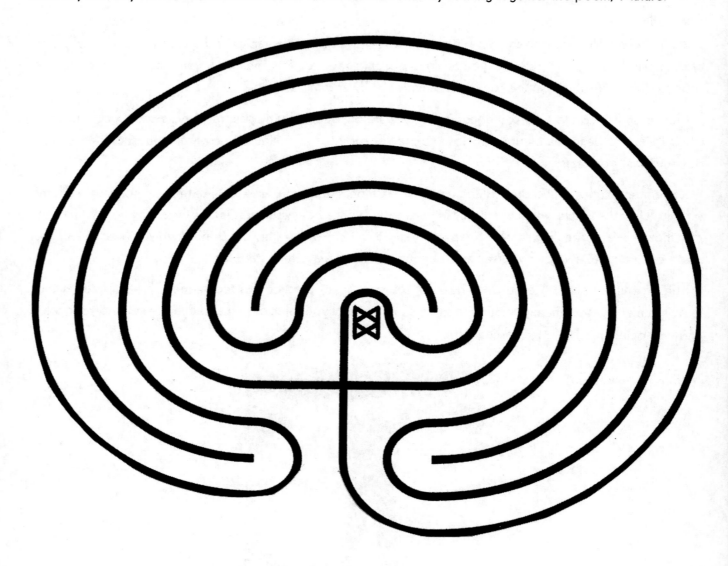

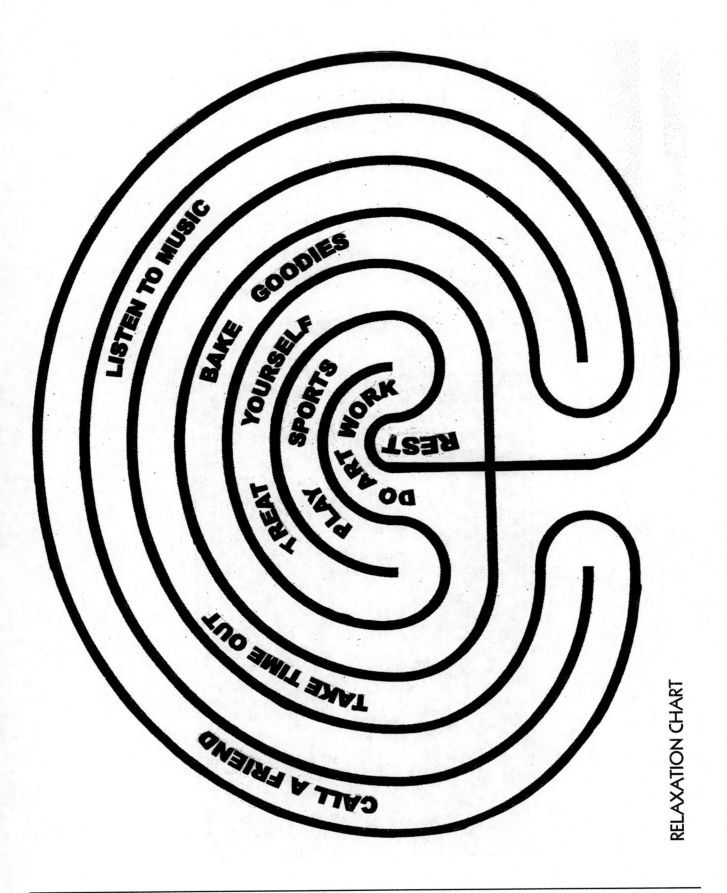

LISTEN TO MUSIC

BAKE GOODIES

YOURSELF

SPORTS

TREAT

PLAY

WORK

DO ART

REST

TAKE TIME OUT

CALL A FRIEND

RELAXATION CHART

NATURE

A TINY WEBBED RAINBOW GLISTENS

A SIGH SOFTLY CRIED

DOES ANYONE HEAR, LISTEN.

A LEAF SLOWLY FALLS

DEEP IN THE FOREST

ITS QUIET WHISPER LINGERS.

A SHAFT OF SUNLIGHT

FOLLOWS THE DUST MOTES

AND WARMS ITSELF IN THE GRASS.

PEACE LABYRINTH WALK CELEBRATION
BACKGROUND INFORMATION - A CULTURE OF VIOLENCE

Violence in our culture has become a way of life. It is found in movies, TV shows and news broadcasts, newspapers, magazines, cartoons, music, video games and sports. Violence reigns among social issues like the death penalty, abortion, crime, domestic violence, drugs, alcohol, gangs, child abuse, the environment and war with nuclear capabilities. At the present time, there are 35 wars taking place across the globe. Even schools, churches and shopping malls are no longer safe.

Violence is so rooted in our society that it becomes the norm, passing it off as, "that's just the way things are". We become desensitized, paralyzed and fearful, thus making violence acceptable. Our indeference supports the culture.

More than ever, building a culture of peace is imperative. The time has come where the responsibility of promoting peace lies with each person. Although no one individual can save the world, if each person promoted peace in his or her corner of the world, there would be no need to save the world. Peace begins by making peace in our hearts first.

VIOLENT LANGUAGE

To create a culture of peace is possible. One suggestion is to begin by cleaning up violent language. Language has a profound affect on the way we live our lives. Become consciously aware of how messages of violence are harmful and destructive. Change violent speech patterns to peaceful alternatives. Try these suggestions. Add to the list violent language you hear in daily conversations.

VIOLENT	NON-VIOLENT
Give it a shot.	Give it a chance.
Not by a long shot	No way.
Shoot for it.	Go for it.
You were going great guns.	You were doing great.
I'm killing time.	I'm waiting until…
Kill two birds with one stone	Doing two things at once.
Nail it down.	Get it right.
She got away with murder.	She sure got away with it.
Take a stab/crack at it.	Try it out.
Have to attack my home work.	Better get started on my homework.
Got to fight for peace.	Work for peace.
The war on cancer.	Trying to cure cancer.
Dance War.	Dance competition.
Strike it from the list.	Erase it from the list.

What is the root cause of destructive language? Perhaps it is because going the way of peace seems weak. Tough is more acceptable. Actually, the opposite is true. Peace takes courage. Some people have paid a high price for peace: Martin Luther King, Jr., Dan Berrigan, Nelson Mandela, Mahatma Gandhi, Mother Teresa, Dorothy Day and the Dalai Lama. Imitate their lives.

DEVELOPMENT OF THE THEME - OTHER WAYS TO BECOME A PEACEFUL PERSON

What is important to remember about making peace is that it begins with the individual person. If each person worked for peace, there would be no violence. Here are other suggestions of making peace.

1. Bring food to a soup kitchen.

2. Tell someone you've hurt that you are sorry.

3. Destroy any war toys or violent games that you own.

4. Accept the things you cannot change.

5. Learn about peoples in other countries. Respect differences.

6. Make friends with someone who is a different race than yours.

7. Stop bullying. Peacefully stick up for those who are bullied.

8. Be happy with those who succeed, avoid jealousy.

9. If you have two of something, give one away.

10. Do something special today for a member of your family.

11. Tell some people you love them.

12. Share a special lunch with someone.

13. Perform a kind act for a classmate.

14. Desire inner peace more than anything else.

15. Play a musical instrument.

16. Find a peaceful space for quiet.

17. Share housekeeping responsibilities in the home.

18. Respect property.

19. Keep your room clean.

20. Listen to peaceful music or music about peace.

21. Set aside a few minutes each day to be quiet.

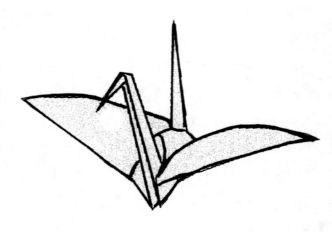

22. Explore your spiritual beliefs.

23. Learn to settle problems by talking instead of fighting.

24. Talk kindly to people instead of using anger or nasty remarks.

25. Refuse to watch violent programs on TV.

26. Create a peace corner in your classroom or home where you can experience peaceful, quiet moments.

27. Acknowledge feelings of frustration, anger and fear.

28. Create a place of beauty in your mind: a flower, birds singing, the sun on your face, etc.

29. Ask questions about things you don't understand.

30. Forgive those who hurt you and ask forgiveness from those you hurt.

31. Be part of a team, play together, volunteer in small groups.

32. Live in the present moment.

33. Believe that war is no way to settle problems. If everyone believed this way, there would be no wars.

34. Take care of your piece of the Earth, the environment where you live.

35. Instead of feeling trapped, accept where you are and move on.

36. Build a peace garden where you reside.

37. Laugh a lot and help others to laugh. Laughter is the best medicine.

38. Know when to walk away from anger.

SADAKO AND THE THOUSAND CRANES

A famous book on peace is *Sadako and the Thousand Cranes* by Eleanor Coerr (Puffin Books). A synopsis of the book is included here.

Ancient legend teaches that your greatest wish will come true if you fold one thousand origami cranes. In 1955, Sadako, a 12-year old Japanese girl, lay dying from radiation sickness 10 years after the bombing in Hiroshima. She undertook to fold 1,000 cranes so that she could live. Sadako also wrote a Haiku (Japanese poem) that read in part: "I shall write peace upon your wings, and you shall fly around the world so that children will no longer have to die this way." Sweet Sadako died before she could complete her task. Her classmates folded the remaining number so that she was buried with One Thousand Cranes.

Ever since, the Origami crane has become recognized worldwide as a symbol of peace and nuclear disarmament. A granite statue of Sadako stands in the Hiroshima Peace Park: a young girl standing with her hand outstretched, a paper crane flying from her fingertips.

THE LABYRINTH WALK ON PEACE

As you walk the labyrinth, think of some of the many ways of promoting peace by using non-violent language or other suggestions given. Choose one you would like to put into practice and decide how you will apply it to your daily life. As you leave the labyrinth, you will be given a crane for peace like the one shown here.

FOLLOW-UP PROCEDURES – WRITING EXERCISE AND DISCUSSION

Write your practice of peace on the back of the crane and hang it on the tree branch secured in a flower pot just outside the labyrinth. Later, display the crane where it can be noticed by all. Conclude the walk by reciting together the Pledge of Non-Violence that follows.

PLEDGE OF NON-VIOLENCE

I WILL RESPECT MYSELF… By avoiding self-destructive behaviors, including the abuse of drugs and alcohol.

I WILL RESPECT OTHERS… By avoiding hateful words, physical or emotional attacks or anything else that would dehumanize them.

I WILL COMMUNICATE BETTER… By sharing my feelings honestly and seeking to understand my anger and ways to express it safely.

I WILL LISTEN… To others, especially those who disagree with me and consider their feelings and needs as important as my own.

I WILL FORGIVE AND SEEK FORGIVENESS… By apologizing to those I hurt, forgiving myself and others and letting go of grudges.

I WILL RESPECT NATURE… By treating all living things with respect, taking care of the environment around me as if it were my own home.

I WILL RECREATE NON-VIOLENTLY… By participating in sports and other activities in ways that show good sportsmanship and refusing to hurt others intentionally.

I WILL BE COURAGEOUS… By challenging violence in all its forms whenever I encounter it, whether at home, in school, at work or the community and by standing with others who are treated unfairly, even if it means standing alone.

> BUILDING A BETTER WORLD
> ONE PERSON AT A TIME,
> STARTING WITH MYSELF.

THE LABYRINTH PEACE SONG

ROUND   **SALLY MARSH, SSJ**

IN   A-ROUND AND   OUT   WE   GO.   IT
WE   ALL SHARE THIS EARTH - LY   SPACE.   YET
DIF-RENT THOUGH OUR JOURNEYS MAY   BE,   WE

MAT - TERS   NOT HOW   FAST   OR   SLOW. WE
SEL - DOM   DO WE   MEET IN   ONE place. WE
SHARE   A   COM-MON   DES -   TIN - Y.   WE

WALK PEACE-FUL LY AS ONE. WE WALK FOR PEACE ON EARTH.

LABYRINTH COMPETENCY BINGO GAME

This is the generic bingo card. Students may be encouraged to make others.

BiNgo

SELF DISCOVERY	MEDITATION	MYSTERY	LIFE'S JOURNEY
PACE	RETURNING	RECEIVING	CIRCUIT
PASS	IN	PORTABLE	PILGRIMAGE
ELEVEN	CIRCULAR	LOST	WRONG
RELEASING	SEVEN	LABYRINTH	RELEASING RECEIVING RETURNING

LABYRINTH BINGO ANSWERS

BiNgo

LOST	4,000	IN	SEVEN
PILGRIMAGE	PORTABLE	WRONG	RELEASING
SELF DISCOVERY	CIRCUIT	MYSTERY	CIRCULAR
RETURNING	RELEASING RECEIVING RETURNING	LIFE'S JOURNEY	PACE
ELEVEN	PASS	MEDITATION	RECEIVING

LABYRINTH COMPETENCY GAME

These questions are used to play the bingo game or used as a written test.

1. The labyrinth is a symbol of _____.

2. The labyrinth path is usually structured in a _____manner.

3. Unlike a maze, you cannot get _____in a labyrinth.

4. The path of the labyrinth is referred to as a _____.

5. The Cretan labyrinth has _____ circuits.

6. The famous _____ circuit labyrinth is found in Chartres Cathedral in France.

7. The way out of the labyrinth is the same as the way _____.

8. In the Middle Ages, people made a _____ to other lands.

9. Labyrinths have been known to exist for about _____ years.

10. The labyrinth is often used as a tool for _____.

11. There is no right or _____ way to walk a labyrinth.

12. The three Rs of the labyrinth are _____.

13. The first R to think about while walking to the center is_____.

14. The R to think about at the center of the labyrinth is _____.

15. The R to think about when leaving the center is _____.

16. The labyrinth is often referred to as a _____.

17. When walking the labyrinth, do it at your own _____.

18. If you meet someone on the path, step aside and let the person _____.

19. A labyrinth carried from place to place is a _____ labyrinth.

20. The labyrinth can be a path to _____.

BINGO GAME ANSWERS

1. life's journey

2. circular

3. lost

4. circuit

5. seven

6. eleven

7. in

8. pilgrimage

9. 4,000 – 6,000

10. meditation

11. wrong

12. releasing, receiving, returning

13. releasing

14. receiving

15. returning

16. mystery

17. pace

18. pass

19. portable

20. self discovery

CONCLUSION

One of the greatest benefits of a teacher's profession is the opportunity to constantly learn. Creative teachers are always alert for new ideas to set the learning process in motion. Teachers aim to capture the minds and interests of students. For this reason, books are teachers' constant companions.

Writing a book for educators is a privilege. Although the author births the book, the educator and student are the ones who continue to give it life.

Education is about making connections; that is, taking what is learned and applying it to other disciplines of learning in order to acquire knowledge and grow more fully as a human being. What better approach is there to learning than to introduce a labyrinth experience? Although a tradition from Ancient times, the labyrinth walk has surfaced to meet the needs of modern times.

The simplicity of the labyrinth experience naturally sparks the interest of students, enabling them to make connections with themselves and the world around them. What greater reward is there for both teacher and student! What greater joy for an author to assist educators in connecting the joy of learning with the fascination of a labyrinth walk. The goal of this book was to explore the answer to these questions.

— Notes —